*"In a time when it seems like everyone in the world is out for themselves and couldn't care less about their impact on others as long as they get what they want, the program is such a breath of fresh air. I cannot recommend the 9 a.m. Meeting enough. You truly get out what you put in. It's an awesome program led by an awesome person."*

—**Lance O.**

*"My attitude at work changed. I was a happier person because I had something I was striving for. I was a more motivated person, wanting nothing but excellence. I was increasing my numbers, which sparked other coworkers to work harder, increasing the store numbers to a new high that I had not seen before. I went into the first meeting not knowing what to expect and ended up changing my life. I owe this company more than words can explain. They have done so much for me, personally and professionally."*

—**Mike W.**

*"I started to realize the amount of time I have is finite. I wonder how long I would have kept doing the same things that weren't leading to my personal success before I would have figured this out. I'm not saying I didn't have grand plans about the things I might want to do before I started the 9 a.m. Meeting… What the 9 a.m. Meeting has helped me to do is draw a map to where I want to be."*

*"What does the 9 a.m. Meeting mean to me? Me time! It's the time where I focus on me and realize what I want out of life and my relationships—when I don't have to be afraid to say I took the wrong path and have the guidance to steer me back on course. To me this meant paying off debt, buying a new home, and having a plan where my financials are concerned... Water-cooler talk is no longer gossip! We are asking what dreams we have accomplished and what we are working on now. We are more confident and productive in our personal lives and are more confident and productive at work!"*

**–Megan L.**

*"There is no better feeling than being able to mark off one of the goals I set for myself. There is a sense of true pride when you can tell someone, 'I'm tackling my dreams.' The program has also inspired me to ask everyone, 'What are your dreams? What are you doing to tackle these dreams?' I enjoy getting those thoughts flowing for every individual. Anything is possible, and I am proud to say I am living proof after losing fifty pounds, and I'm maintaining my current weight, paying off all my bad debt, working toward being a better person all around, and this is just the tip of the iceberg! I want my legacy to be as rich and as positive as possible, and I am well on my way! Are you?"*

**–Mike S.**

# The 9 a.m. Meeting

# The 9 a.m. Meeting

A high-impact approach to making work
meaningful, energizing employees, and
taming the turnover tiger

DOUG ECKLUND

Published by Advantage, Charleston, South Carolina.
Member of Advantage Media Group.

ADVANTAGE is a registered trademark and the Advantage colophon is a trademark of Advantage Media Group, Inc.

Printed in the United States of America.

ISBN: 978-1-59932-513-2
LCCN: 2016939822

Book design by Katie Biondo.

This publication is designed to provide accurate and authoritative information in regard to the subject matter covered. It is sold with the understanding that the publisher is not engaged in rendering legal, accounting, or other professional services. If legal advice or other expert assistance is required, the services of a competent professional person should be sought.

Advantage Media Group is proud to be a part of the Tree Neutral® program. Tree Neutral offsets the number of trees consumed in the production and printing of this book by taking proactive steps such as planting trees in direct proportion to the number of trees used to print books. To learn more about Tree Neutral, please visit **www.treeneutral.com.** To learn more about Advantage's commitment to being a responsible steward of the environment, please visit **www.advantagefamily.com/green**

Advantage Media Group is a publisher of business, self-improvement, and professional development books and online learning. We help entrepreneurs, business leaders, and professionals share their Stories, Passion, and Knowledge to help others Learn & Grow. Do you have a manuscript or book idea that you would like us to consider for publishing? Please visit **advantagefamily.com** or call **1.866.775.1696.**

*In loving memory of my parents, William J. and Jane F. Ecklund, who modeled the servant's heart to me.*

*To my warrior wife Mitzi and kiddos Natalie and Will. Because of you I know the joy of unconditional love, family, and faith in a greater future.*

*To Nick Villotti for having the courage to bloom where he was planted and all the lives he has invested in and positively impacted.*

*And finally, to my Heavenly Father, giver of grace and second chances!*

# TABLE OF CONTENTS

# ACKNOWLEDGMENTS

This book would not have made it into print without the love, encouragement, competence, and support of many people. I am grateful to all those who provided an encouraging word or kick in the tail and who brought their own gifts and talents to this project.

To Tom Allen—friend, entrepreneur, leader, and connector of people—for helping get me off square one.

To my YPO forum mates for not allowing me to have another reason this wasn't getting done. Love you my brothers!

To the cast of characters in our Island of Misfit Toys at Cellular Advantage for supporting this work during a time of growth.

Finally, to my friends and family who have reviewed titles, cover designs, and content, your input and ability to see into my blind spots has been so valuable!

# INTRODUCTION
## SEEKING SIGNIFICANCE

This book tells our story at Cellular Advantage, Inc. and shares the tools we use to invest in our people and reduce employee turnover in our organization. It contains some timeless truths, things we learned along the way, and the tools we blended together to create a process that can take someone from reacting to life to pursuing life and being excited about their life, work, and goals.

The processes and tools we use today didn't just materialize overnight. The success we enjoy today is the result of the experiences we've had along the way. The backstory will shed some light on that.

I was living the entrepreneurial dream. I had a growing company, and I was living for myself, feeding the ego—becoming a "big deal." My purpose of being in business was to make a lot of money and become a big deal. That is what it was to me for the first ten years. That led to a company and marriage that were both just hanging on. That way of doing things stopped in 2004 when I found myself looking over a cliff, wondering what this world would say if I were gone. I thought about it enough that I wrote it down. I literally wrote my own eulogy as if I had died in the summer of 2004. I had made a mess of our company and was failing at my marriage. I was probably one phone call away from either or both of them coming to an end.

Then I wrote a second eulogy. This one was about a man who lived until he was old, finished strong, and lived a life of *significance*. That eulogy helped shape my marriage and our company going forward.

It was the new North Star. It boiled down to one word.

**Significance:** *The quality of having a meaning. Having or likely to have influence or effect.*

How could my life become a life of significance?

How could our company become a company of significance? This question helped shape our company's purpose statement and core values. It gave us a "why" for getting up every day.

Our purpose at Cellular Advantage is "To enrich the quality of life for our own and our customers at each interaction." When we do the first part for our staff, interestingly enough, then the same tends to happen for our customers.

We have the ability to enrich the quality of life of our own—the people we hire and trust to execute our goals. That is where it started in our company. That purpose statement gave Nick Villotti, VP of Sales, the green light to start meeting with staff, asking questions, and mostly listening, to learn how we could inspire our employees to get excited about achieving their own goals. This practice of regularly engaging with employees eventually turned into the 9 a.m. Meeting. During this standing meeting, Nick learned that many of our staff members were letting life come at them rather than taking control of their lives and dreams. They were just existing. He also saw that what was coming at them in their personal lives consistently carried over to the workplace. This is one of the truths we've learned along the way: **quality of life on the personal side is directly related to quality of life on the work side.**

Investing in people and enriching their quality of life through the 9 a.m. Meeting evolved into a more formal series of meetings and questions that makes up the *what* part of the book, in chapters 3–6. But that is just one small part of our story. Read on for the rest of it, and use this book as a tool to impact turnover and make your business—and your life—significant.

# PART I

## A COMPANY'S
## TRANSFORMATION

# CHAPTER 1

## THE START-UP

My wife, Mitzi, graduated from college and took an inside sales job with U.S. Cellular, the carrier we have worked with since day one, in the early 1990s. In 1992, Mitzi was one of their top performers, in the top 4 percent, which meant she was in their President's Club.

U.S. Cellular operated a kiosk in Southridge Mall on the south side of Des Moines, Iowa. At that time, there were three malls in Des Moines, and Southridge Mall would have been considered the least fancy of the three. It was fairly full of businesses, but it was not thriving. U.S. Cellular decided that financially it would make more sense for them to have an authorized agent operate the kiosk than to continue to operate it themselves.

So they approached Mitzi and offered her the opportunity to become an authorized agent for U.S. Cellular. Accepting the opportunity, Mitzi incorporated Cellular Advantage in 1993 as an authorized agent of U.S. Cellular. Historically, U.S. Cellular's customers have been acquired approximately fifty-fifty between their company-owned stores and authorized-agent locations like Cellular Advantage.

I had a job in the financial-services industry at the time. Mitzi and I were engaged to be married. She came to me and asked what I thought. I said the thought of being in business for yourself sounded great. She talked to her dad. He has been an entrepreneurial spirit his whole life, and his comment was, "You are twenty-three years old, why wouldn't you? If the thing doesn't work, go back out into the workforce and get another job."

I called my district manager at the financial-services company I was working for and told him I was going to take a month off to help my fiancee start a business and asked him to handle my accounts. We were running Lotus 1–2–3 software on a computer with a black-and-white screen, trying to work on a business plan that we would then print and fax down to Mitzi's dad in Florida. He'd take a look at it, make some notes on it, and fax it back to us. What different times those were.

I look back at those times now and kind of laugh about how we operated. Cellular Advantage would buy equipment from different vendors. For example, Cellular Advantage would buy a bag phone for one hundred dollars. When activating service with U.S. Cellular, the customer would get the phone for free. Cellular Advantage would earn a commission from U.S. Cellular for activating the service, but this commission, depending on what time of the month it was, would not be received for thirty to sixty days after the date of the activation.

This cash-flow model got some pretty funny looks and comments from the banks we were looking to borrow money from. All we wanted to borrow was $35,000. It was not a huge loan. It was a big deal to us at the time but not to a bank. Even so, no one wanted to loan us the money. We finally found a bank that was willing to do it, but in order to minimize the bank's risk, she had to put her car up as collateral against the loan.

We moved out of our one-bedroom apartment and into a two-bedroom apartment so that we could have an office, which was comprised of a used photocopy machine and a giant old IBM computer. We stored our inventory in that room as well because the kiosk did not have much storage space. We started with a few people in that little apartment, and our first day with a store at Southridge Mall was tax day, April 15, 1993. We added a second store in Valley West Mall later that year. A good month of sales at a mall kiosk back then would be fifteen phones. It was not yet a retail product, but we were moving ahead as if it were.

I think we were a little ahead of ourselves in opening those retail stores. Most sales came from our direct salespeople. Cellular Advantage had a half dozen salespeople out in the field. They were calling on contractors and attorneys, professionals and blue-collar guys—anyone who was out working in any capacity—and trying to sell phones via a direct sales model.

That was how we were able to survive those first few years. The $35,000 was gone pretty quickly, so we started filling out credit card applications. Mitzi and I had several credit cards each, which were quickly maxed out. We were trying to just get by in any way we could and were struggling, to say the least.

The two mall stores were open from 10:00 a.m. until 9:00 p.m., six days a week, and then on Sundays from noon until 5:00 p.m. We were always working, whether that meant opening the stores, being there during the day, or going there at 9:00 p.m. to close them and make sure the cash got to the bank. There was almost no downtime. During that time I also learned how to install phones. Removing and installing phones was a big part of the industry in the earlier years, and it paid pretty well too.

Cellular Advantage worked with the local Sam's Club, where we were able to set up a table and sell phones from there—an arrangement that linked a Sam's Club membership with a free phone. If you renewed your Sam's Club membership, you got a certificate for a free phone from our company. We moved quite a few phones out of Sam's Club back in the day. That was a lot of fun.

Unfortunately, we got to a point where our credit cards were all maxed out and the bank had lent us all that they were going to lend us. We could see that we were going to have a hard time making payroll in the coming months, so we borrowed a little money from my mom and dad and put my Jeep up for sale. We let the Jeep go in a "fire sale" kind of way—really cheap. It was not a good transaction, but it got us some cash. I paid back my parents the couple thousand they had lent us, and I used the rest of the money to make payroll.

Around this time, my in-laws were nice enough to lend us a car to use. It was named "the Woody." It was a Chrysler K car station wagon with wood paneling on the sides. Clark W. Griswold would have been proud. There was always a race at our house in the morning to be the first one out so that you would not have to drive the Woody. That thing was a little better than the first car I had when I was a kid, but not much. No one wanted to drive the Woody. It became part of our history and part of our story, which now is kind of fun.

Mitzi and I got married in July of 1993 in Peoria, Illinois, and wanted to go on at least a little bit of a honeymoon, but we still had the stores to look after. My in-laws, who live in Florida, said, "Come down and stay at our house, and we'll watch the stores for you in Des Moines while you are gone." We took them up on their offer and enjoyed some relaxing time together for the first time in a long time. After a nice walk on the beach, we decided to call Mitzi's dad and check in.

Mitzi's dad had been an entrepreneur all his life. He had owned several businesses. We felt good having him in the driver's seat. So we called him and said, "How's everything going?" "Everything is fine up here, but I did have to fire a guy this morning." That one shook us a little bit, I have to say. Now we can look back at it and laugh, but at the time it sent our stress levels through the roof. We soon got back to Des Moines and back to work. There were often struggles and stress, but somehow we made it through those first three years.

Work was not our only source of stress and struggle. Even our social life was working against us. Or maybe we were working against it. Either way, it was a problem. Mitzi and I have always had great friends, and thankfully we still do. But back when we were struggling with our young business, our friends stopped calling because our reply was always "We've got to be at work," or "We've got to close the store," or some variation of that.

With all the hours we were working, there was not a whole lot of breathing room. At the same time, if we were going to go out and do something, it was probably going to have to be put on a credit card because we were light on cash. So our saying no over and over probably was a combination of both those things. But even if we did have the cash to spend, we were open seven days a week, and it was just the two of us. That does not leave much time for happy hour.

We moved out of the two-bedroom apartment and into a rental house in 1996, which gave us a little more room. There was a full-blown office in that house, in addition to the two retail stores. Even so, I would not say that things were going a whole lot better than they had been in the cramped apartment. The first winter that we were in the house, we started noticing little black pebbles in our kitchen.

11

We figured out pretty soon that they were "presents" that a family of mice had been leaving for us. Ultimately, we had to store all of our dishes and silverware in the refrigerator just to keep them clean and sanitary. We had a proper office but were infested with mice.

I vividly remember watching TV one night and seeing a mouse run right across the living room floor. Our dog was so freaked out that she jumped up onto the couch with us. Next thing I knew, I was on the phone with the exterminators. They came out and told us the bad news; we had a "significant" amount of mice in our house that came in via a crack in the foundation. We knew we had to figure out a way to make some money so that we could get out of there and buy a home of our own.

So we started working more and socializing even less. One of our friends decided to check in and ask how things were going. I said, "Things aren't going that great." She said that her father-in-law, Steve Stahly, might be a good guy to talk to. I knew him because he was on an Ernst & Young phone plan, and I had tried to sell him a phone. He'd said, "No, I'm getting this special rate through these guys." I thought he was an accountant because he was affiliated with the Ernst & Young phone plan.

Mitzi and I went to Steve's kitchen, sat down, and started talking. I said, "I really appreciate you meeting with us to try to help us get this figured out. It's great to have an accountant on the scene." He looked at me and said, "I'm not an accountant." I said, "I thought you were because you've got an Ernst & Young phone."

"No," he said. "Those guys do work for me, and part of our deal is that they provide me with a phone."

"Oh," I said. "What do you do?"

"I'm a business owner," he said.

And that is how our relationship with Steve Stahly began, with that simple exploratory conversation. We came to find out that he owned several companies and that he was on the board of directors of a few more.

He said, "Doug, a business owner needs to talk to a business owner. You need to have an accountant. You need to have an attorney. You need to have people with those sets of skills, but ultimately, the best place to get advice on how to run a business is from another business owner."

We returned to his kitchen table several times over the course of many months. He helped us dive into our financial statements and make sense of them. He helped us figure out how we did things and which of those things we were doing right. We learned so much from him.

He helped us change so many things, but he did it in little bite-size chunks. When he gave us homework, we would go and execute it and then come back two weeks later. We would sit down and tell him what we had accomplished and then talk it over, and he would give us another project. Everything built on the prior thing, and it was all very digestible and manageable. A tremendous amount was learned from him, little by little. As Cellular Advantage grew to six locations in the Des Moines area, we knew things needed to be more systematized and more simple. Mitzi and I wanted to try to keep everything as easy as possible for our employees so that they did not have to worry about the details—so they could just focus on serving the customer.

We were really trying to work on the business and make the business something that was sustainable. If Mitzi and I wanted to go on vacation for a week, we wanted the store to operate as if we were there, as if there were no difference to the customer. That was really the goal.: to free up our own time because we had done nothing but work darn near every day for quite a few years. We were trying to transition from "having a job" to "being business owners."

In late 1996, the cellular industry started to move more toward retail. People began buying cell phones as a convenience item as compared to having them only for work. So the retail stores started to get busier, and things started to change slowly for the better.

Right around that time, Cellular Advantage was approached by new wireless carriers. Sprint came to the Des Moines market, so we added Sprint. Shortly after that, Nextel came to the Des Moines market, so we added Nextel's products. And shortly after that, AT&T came, and then T-Mobile.

Cellular Advantage ended up with five of the six carriers that were represented in Des Moines. So as a company, things had to get more organized. We had to start acting more like a big company and less like a husband and wife running a couple of retail stores.

That was a game changer for us because we got to see our quality of life improve. We grew the business enough that we were eligible to be a part of an organization called YEO, Young Entrepreneurs' Organization. My wife's father had been in YPO, which is Young Presidents' Organization. YEO and YPO are kind of brother/sister organizations. So he recommended that we join YEO, but there wasn't a chapter in Iowa at that time, so Mitzi joined the St. Louis chapter and started making a monthly trip down there.

Mitzi would go down and meet with other business owners in a small group setting, and we would sometimes both go to listen to different speakers on leadership and a variety of other topics. Listening to those talks really helped us to become better leaders at our company. In 1997, our banker nominated Mitzi for an Ernst and Young Entrepreneur of the Year Award, which was available to business owners in Iowa, Nebraska, and Kansas, and Mitzi and Cellular Advantage won that award for our category. It was a great honor, especially considering where we had been just a few years before. To be recognized as a company that was doing a good job was pretty cool—a huge morale boost.

By then, there were a number of processes in place to make the business run. If Mitzi and I were not there, we knew the reporting was there to show us what happened in our absence.

YEO is a great organization for learning. At YEO events, you usually end up across the table from somebody who has faced the same things you have. They might operate an entirely different kind of business, but at some point they have probably dealt with a similar issue to what you are facing. When you sit down together, you just end up sharing ideas. It is impossible not to. The whole concept there is continual learning, continual education via the sharing of personal experiences. That organization was tremendously valuable and important to us, to our success.

It also got me into some personal trouble. There were a lot of people in the organization who ran pretty hard socially, and their priorities were very much to just grow, grow, grow the business. They were of the mind-set that *I'm going to work a million hours a week, and that's really the only thing that matters to me. I'm not going to be home that much. My priority is work and myself, personally.* I was exposed to a lot of that right around the time we were having our first child, and unfortunately, I got caught up in it myself.

After our daughter was born, Mitzi decided that she was going to step partway out of the business and be home for our child, Natalie. Mitzi had joined the YEO organization first, and she was most involved with it in the beginning. So instead of driving down to St. Louis myself for YEO functions, Mitzi and I realized that we knew enough people in Des Moines to get a YEO chapter going. We started a local YEO chapter in 2000, and twenty-three people joined right out of the gate.

YEO is just a great organization, but as I alluded to earlier, I got swept up in it. I started believing what all those other "work hard, play hard" business owners were saying. I started telling myself, "I'm going to work my tail off, and then I'm going to go have as much fun as I can with all of my buddies." Well, that made me more of an absentee husband and father than anything else. So my priorities were not in the right place in those years, 2000 through 2003, and even into 2004. My priorities were off, and I was not doing myself, my family, or even my business any good.

In 2002, we were told by the local U.S. Cellular office that Jay Ellison, the executive vice president of U.S. Cellular, wanted to come to town and meet us.

We met with him at our main office, where he pitched us on an opportunity to grow our company with U.S. Cellular.

Jay told us that once U.S. Cellular completed its acquisition of PrimeCo in Chicago later in the year, they would need agent distribution in Chicago and would like for Cellular Advantage to come and open stores in Chicago.

We later learned that Cellular Advantage was one of only four companies selected from a group of more than four hundred U.S. Cellular dealers in the country to open stores in Chicago. Looking back on it, it was a pretty big honor to be picked. I guess we were doing something right!

But the deal that Jay put in front of us was daunting—he wanted Cellular Advantage to become a national agent. This meant meeting the requirement of having twenty-five locations operating in four different U.S. Cellular markets.

Jay then went on to reveal the other requirement: *making this happen over a period of twelve months.* "In exchange for all of this, we're going to support you to help make this all happen," he said. "We want you to come to Chicago. We're also going to be launching the Omaha market in the spring of next year. We'd like to see you go over there, too. So what do you think?"

This was very exciting, and I could feel the excitement inside me. We had an opportunity to grow our company with their assistance. I was sitting there saying to myself, *Holy cow, I'm running around with all of these other entrepreneurs who have got their own growth strategies, and they're really shooting for the moon. Well, here's our chance to shoot for the moon, too.*

In YEO, a big deal is to make the Inc. 500 list—the five hundred fastest-growing companies in the United States. We had grown each year for the previous few years, but if we did this, our year-end 2002 was going to be a significant increase over 2001. And then in 2003, when we got the rest of the stores opened up, it would again result in huge growth over the previous year. We were going to make the Inc. 500 list. I remember thinking, *This is going to be so cool.* I could see our name on that list, and my ego started to inflate from the moment we had that meeting with Jay.

We got back together with Steve Stahly and told him what we were expected to achieve in the given time frame and that we were considering it—but we wanted his advice. With Steve's help, we built a financial model, a business plan detailing how to proceed in this new arrangement. We showed that around to three different banks, and eventually we found one that wanted to do this deal with us. From our point of view, we had borrowed a lot of money. To other companies, it might not be that big of a deal, but we had a couple million dollars available to us to do this growth plan. And that was a lot of money to us. *A lot.*

We hit the "go" button, and the clock started ticking. The race was on—the race to get to twenty-five stores in four states. The first thing Cellular Advantage did was go to Joplin, Missouri. Nick Villotti, who I have already mentioned, was with us in a direct-sales function at that point. We scheduled a meeting with him and said, "Nick, we need somebody to go run the three stores that we are going to open down in the Joplin area. Are you up for it?" He said yes, and he moved with his daughter to Joplin. Nick was in charge of getting the Joplin stores going. He would also prove to be a huge asset in another aspect of our company—one of the most important innovations we have ever incorporated—and we will get to that later.

Once Joplin was established, our next task was to try to get things done in Chicago—to be open there when U.S. Cellular was ready to launch. They were going to try to launch in Chicago on Black Friday of 2002. So I went to the Windy City time and time again. I spent a tremendous amount of time there trying to find real estate, trying to get leases finalized, and trying to get stores built and open. I'm a small-town Iowa guy, and I was going into downtown Chicago, a place I had visited only a couple of times as a tourist, and I was trying to make real estate decisions. I didn't realize it at the time, but I was a fish out of water.

Here is a great example. I was in Chicago with a real estate agent. I got in his car and drove around downtown. He pulled up in front of a space that was available for lease and he said, "This is one of my 'A' locations, one of the best spots I've got to show you today. Here's why this looks so good." And he went on to tell me all of the great things about the property. I looked at it. There were a few parallel parking spots on the street in front of it. Obviously there was no parking lot because it was downtown Chicago. Before going to Chicago, my leaders and I had built a checklist of the characteristics of our top stores, and this location didn't have any of them.

I told him, "Well, this doesn't make any sense. Where do people park? And the signage doesn't look very good. I just don't see how this thing's going to work. If this is an 'A' location, I'm really confused." The agent probably thought I was the biggest idiot. He said, "A train drops off right over here, one block to the left. And every day thousands of people will walk right past your front door going to and from that particular train. They don't have a car, so you don't have to worry about the parking lot. And your sign's going to be right here. They're going to be walking right underneath it. You can put some things in the front windows—light boxes and things like that." He took me through about four different reasons why this was a great location. And that is when I really figured out that I didn't know what I was doing in downtown Chicago.

Things went from bad to worse as we were trying to get locations signed and opened in time for Black Friday. As far as the permitting process goes, I was used to Des Moines. When we were going to build out a store, we would go to the city, fill out the necessary forms, and within a week or two, the construction could start.

In Chicago, we learned it could take *eight* weeks or more just to get a permit. Eight weeks! From there, there were so many different hoops that you had to jump through and so many different things that had to happen just to get a store open. There were ten leases signed, and by Black Friday, only two were open. It was largely due to our lack of knowledge about the whole process of doing business in Chicago.

It was a big mess because there really wasn't any vision as to how this was going to happen. It was a big land grab. There were three other agents besides Cellular Advantage opening stores in Chicago, plus the corporate U.S. Cellular stores they were going to open. Our stores ended up being stretched clear across the suburbs, from as far south as Orland Park up north into the Crystal Lake area, out west to Naperville, and then back east to downtown. There was no rhyme or reason to where we ended up having stores in the Chicago area. It was just wherever we could make them happen because in the back of my mind, I knew we needed to be at twenty-five by June 1.

Throughout that whole process I was never home. I had a wife who was not getting any support or any attention, and we had a newborn. I was working all day, then going out and drinking after work, and then getting up and doing it again the next day. The company was growing at a pace that, in hindsight, was out of control. The couple of million dollars that we had borrowed from the bank had been quickly gobbled up. Cellular Advantage was in trouble—*I was in trouble.*

We got to the point in 2003 where the Chicagoland stores were finally open. Then the focus transitioned from Chicago to Omaha because five more stores were needed to get to twenty-five. The Omaha launch happened on June 1, so we made it within a year and met the requirements of the contract. Barely.

By then Cellular Advantage had run out of money. With Steve Stahly's guidance, I figured out that some more expertise on the accounting side of things was needed, so we hired a CFO, Matt, who started in the summer of 2003. He and I had weekly conversations discussing how we could get things back on track. Matt was cleaning up mess after mess. He really managed the relationship well with the bank because we were literally one phone call away from the bank shutting us down. Cellular Advantage was out of compliance on a few of the loan covenants, and I was personally out of compliance on who knows how many things in my marriage. Literally, the business and my marriage were each probably a phone call away from just being done.

If you want to look at a turning point for our company and me personally, this was it. It was 2004, and the whole thing was just a huge mess. I could visualize standing on a cliff looking down. It was a pretty long way down, and I was able to get a really clear picture of what things would look like if I were to fall over the edge. I felt my stomach turn upside down and go up into my throat. It was pretty scary. It was a big wake-up call. I wrote my own eulogy as if I had fallen over the cliff that day.

I said to myself, *What if I'm gone tomorrow? What are people going to say about me?* I wrote that eulogy, and it was, to put it bluntly, brutal. The first thing that I wrote down was, "Who's going to actually get up and say something about this guy who made such a big mess of his life and his company? He's got 120 employees who are all potentially without jobs now. He's got a wife and kids who are without a father. Who's going to say anything about this guy? And who's going to actually show up at this thing?" My life was a mess. And writing out that eulogy and really being honest with myself about how my life was at that moment was a wake-up call. It helped save my business and my marriage. It saved my life.

The process was so eye opening and helpful that after I got all of the junk out of my system, I sat down and wrote a second eulogy— written as if I had finished my life strong, at ninety years old, and finally ran out of gas. That second eulogy pondered the question: If I lived the rest of my life completely differently than I had been, what would people say about me then? After I wrote the second eulogy, I looked at it quarterly just to ask myself, "Do my calendar and my actions match up with what I want people to remember about me when it's all over?"

# Eulogy

*Here lies Doug.*

*He was a strong, caring, compassionate man who loved God and loved people.*

*He was someone who "walked the talk." Those of you who knew him knew that his "talk" or key word that gave him a reason to rise every day was* **significance***. That word was carried out in his daily actions. He enjoyed challenging people to develop and grow, and I would say he impacted many lives in this role as a gardener of people. He saw people for who they could be, not for who they may have been.*

*He was a giver.*

*He knew what it meant to be a great friend.*

*He knew the meaning of love and how to express it in ways that were unique to each of those who were close to him.*

*He was always a joy to be around. He was one of my exceptionally inspiring people. Whenever I was feeling down, I knew that I could count on him for a little pick-me-up or some wisdom that would calm my stress level. I could only hope to have his sense of peace.*

*Most importantly, his gardening showed in his relationships at home. His wife and children will miss him dearly. He learned that to make a marriage truly special, it required daily investments. He learned that to be a great husband you should love your wife in an understanding way, an active way. His marriage was richly fulfilling. His children were well prepared for life, and each had a good understanding of their unique strengths and gifts as they left the home. They both attribute much of their success and passion in and for life to how they were raised at home.*

*He will be missed.*

That was a really big turning point for me. Most importantly, it was a turning point at home, as far as being a good husband and a good father went. And on the company side of things, it ultimately led us in 2005 to write a purpose statement for our company. Why are we in business? What's truly the reason we are doing this? It got us to write our core values. What do we stand for? No matter what is going on in the industry or in other business sectors, what are the principles that Cellular Advantage is going to stand on, no matter what? What are the things that matter to the customer that also set us apart from our competitors? The answers to these questions would allow us to write a brand promise.

The leadership team got together and worked through the questions, and we came out of it with clear answers. It was just a completely different way of leading, both on the personal side and the professional side of my life.

The purpose statement for Cellular Advantage is: **to enrich the quality of life for our own and our customers at each interaction.** Our own is intentionally first in that statement because if we can help enrich the quality of life for our staff members, the fact that they are in a better place personally translates into better store morale, which leads to an awesome customer experience. Enrich is defined as "improve or enhance the quality or value of."

Phones, which were once a luxury item, are now considered essential. Cell phones are lifelines for people. They allow people to stay in touch with everything. While our industry was a luxury starting out, we now have the opportunity to significantly enrich the quality of life for our customers. But the staff comes first because they are our people, and they are very important to us. If we can serve our staff, they are going to be much more likely to serve our customers.

Our core values are also very simple.

1.  **Encourage and respect personal initiative and creativity.**
    Our staff should feel that they can tell us anything. They
    should feel that they can approach us with any idea they
    have. Creativity is important to us. We want them to be
    problem solvers, people who don't stop at roadblocks but
    show resolve to find a way. There are no bad ideas. Any
    person who will be on the leadership team at Cellular
    Advantage won't be afraid to admit there may be a better
    way than their way.

2.  **First understand, then be understood.** This concept is
    from Stephen Covey's book *The 7 Habits of Highly Successful
    People*, and we adopted it as one of our core values because
    it's important to be good listeners. That is what it really
    boils down to. Let's listen and let's understand what is going
    on before we start talking. The real source of this core value
    (and maybe Covey's quotation) is Proverbs 18:13.

3.  **Excellence in reputation by exceeding expectations of
    customers and employees.** Cellular Advantage wants to
    build its good reputation by exceeding expectations. To
    put it another way, we try to underpromise and overdeliver.
    This applies to the personal side of life, too. King Solomon
    wrote in Proverbs 22:1, "Choose a good reputation over
    great riches, for being held in high esteem is better than
    having silver or gold."

4.  **Have fun!** We want our work environment to be something
    that is unique, different—a fun place to work, where there
    is laughter, and people are ribbing each other and just
    having a great time. I think that is something that has
    allowed us to retain people as well. When it is fun to go to

work, people tend to keep working there. There is scripture at Ecclesiastes 8:15 and Proverbs 17:22 that provides the foundation for fun.

Our brand promise is twofold, since we actually serve two different customers. We serve the customers who visit our stores looking for wireless phones and services, and we also serve U.S. Cellular, who pays us for getting these customers.

Cellular Advantage's brand promise to U.S. Cellular is **"Your targets are our guarantees."** We want them to view our company as the "most sought-out agent," the one that they call first whenever they need anything done.

Our brand promise to the customer who visits our stores is **"No surprises. We walk in your shoes!"** We feel that this sentiment really matters to our customers, and it differentiates us from our competitors. Knowing the significance of what we do, really understanding someone and what they need is so important to building a long-term relationship with them. Our staff tries to learn as much as possible about every customer.

In our exclusive five-step needs-analysis process, we ask the right kinds of questions. Is this a budget play for them? Are they going to use this device to watch movies? The process allows us to find out and walk in their shoes. The customer is kept informed. Our customers should not be surprised about anything. They should not be surprised when they open their bill. They should not be surprised when they try to do something on their device that they think it can do but actually it cannot. They should understand everything and expect the best of everything because "we walk in their shoes."

That is what we came up with after looking out over the edge of the cliff—when we decided to do things differently as a company. Instead of just saying, "Let's make the Inc. 500 list, make a bunch of money, and have a great time partying," we recognized that there is something bigger. This isn't just a cell phone business; our company can **enrich the quality of life of those we come in contact with on a daily basis**. We can deliver on our promises and be faithful to a higher ideal.

And that new way of thinking gave birth to an even bigger concept. It was named *The 9 a.m. Meeting*, and it has changed the lives of many people.

# Chapter One Takeaways:

- This was a true start-up, not only as businesspeople but also with the product we were selling, as cell phones had not yet come into their own.
- We made a lot of silly mistakes that young, inexperienced people make, and I made some pretty big mistakes myself.
- We got in over our heads, specifically with the national agent opportunity.
- My business and marriage were one phone call away from ending.
- In using the eulogy to help change the "why," things turned around at work and at home.

# CHAPTER 2

## THE START OF
## SOMETHING BIG

Throughout the whole debacle, when things figuratively went south, Nick Villotti was there for us. If you recall, he literally went south and took one for the team by directing the sales of our three stores down in Joplin, Missouri. During the rocky year of 2004, Nick came to us and said, "Hey, I want to come back to Des Moines to be closer to my family."

The timing could not have worked out better. We actually needed somebody to come in and run the Des Moines market—and Nick was the right guy to do it. Nick moved back to Des Moines in early fall of 2004.

As we moved into the second half of 2005 and our purpose statement—**To enrich the quality of life for our own and our customers at each interaction**—our core values, and our brand promise were formulated, Nick and I started talking about how we could consciously and regularly demonstrate our ideals in our everyday actions.

Nick's currency is seeing people come alive by growing and becoming better people. He was thinking about what he could do to better invest in people. Nick was looking at our purpose statement, and he started thinking, *I've got a lot of people here who just seem like they're taking whatever life is throwing at them, and that's it.* So he started a conversation with one person and said, "What do you want out of life?" and what he got back was a blank stare. So Nick started thinking about this idea more, and he said to himself, *How can I start asking that question in a way that will produce an answer? How can I invest my time and energy in our employees' lives? If I figure that out, then maybe they will open up, and we can help them stop reacting to life and start pursuing something.*

So he literally taped a piece of paper to his door and wrote "9 a.m. meeting" on it, and the 9 a.m. Meeting was born. The idea was that any employee could come in and sign up for a time to talk. Monday, Tuesday, Wednesday, Thursday, Friday. At nine a.m., Nick's door was open. Sign your name on the sheet, and come in and talk to Nick.

Close to ten years later, he still starts those meetings the same way:

*Hey, first things first. Number one, I don't expect you to work here forever. I want you to know that. I assume that at some point down the road, in the future, you're probably going to go off and do something else. I want to help you become the best version of you that you can be when it's time for you to go. Because when you're at your next job or in the next phase of your life, somebody's going to be like, "Well, why are you like that? What's different about you?" or "What is it about you?", and you can just look at them and say, "I'm the way I am because of my experience at Cellular Advantage and the 9 a.m. Meeting."*

The meetings started off just as informal conversations about life, and Nick started to pick up on a few themes pretty early on. Some people were struggling with debt, specifically credit-card debt. "How do I pay for a car?" they'd say. They had various things they wanted to do and accomplish but with no grasp on how they were to do so in regard to expenses. Nick started bringing me these stories. And these things started tugging on my heart just like they were on Nick's heart, too. It is just amazing how the whole process evolved.

Our people were introduced to Financial Peace University (which has since evolved into a program called Smart Dollar), a tool we were exposed to at church. The program is a perfect fit for our people. There is an online version of Financial Peace University, and it was made available to our staff. The cost was $100. The cost was split fifty-fifty with them. Anyone who finished the program would get their $50 back. We wanted to give them as much incentive as possible as motivation to fully participate and succeed.

Gas prices were going all over the place back then. Nick gave our employees a tool that helped them truly understand where their money went each week. When gas would go down a dollar per gallon, they would know that $50 a month was just found, and that $50 could go toward paying a credit card off. Through Financial Peace University, Nick had lots of different tools to offer our people.

Men's Fraternity, a group that Nick and I were involved in at the time, offered a definition of an "authentic man," and it became something that we actually worked into our employee-review process. An authentic man is someone who accepts responsibility, rejects passivity, leads courageously, has a great attitude, and expects a great reward. And that is something that Nick worked into the 9 a.m. meeting as well.

In the 9 a.m. Meeting, he decided to start talking to people about not being passive, because most people were just sitting back taking what life threw at them, and they were not actually moving toward something. They were not pursuing anything. He talked to them about accepting responsibility. Nick heard a lot of people talking about being victims as opposed to accepting responsibility for the situation that they were in and accepting the responsibility of getting themselves out of that situation.

Our people are encouraged to be courageous leaders. "If you're married," we told them, "you can be a courageous leader as a husband or wife. You can be a courageous leader as a mom or dad or as an employee in your store." Nick talked to our people about attitudes and expecting good things to happen. He said, "If you are going to do these things—be a courageous leader and accept responsibility and pursue your dreams—let's have a great attitude about it and expect a great reward at the end of it."

Nick and I started talking about different things that we had experienced in our own lives because we are not immune to the challenges everyone else faces. We just happened to be a little older and more experienced than many of our employees. Our life experiences already included much of what they were currently going through. Nick figured out how to introduce those things into the 9 a.m. Meeting, and soon the results came. People were getting out of debt. People were growing personally, setting goals, and achieving them. People were buying houses with an appropriate down payment instead of with the "zero down" fiasco that a lot of people unfortunately got duped into. Someone paid cash for an engagement ring.

There were all kinds of really cool stories—all as a result of the 9 a.m. Meeting. We were thinking, *Hey, this is working.*

So Nick would sit down and have these conversations with people, and then he would come down to my office and give me an overview of how things were going. As it evolved and gained popularity among our employees and produced very real results, it turned into more of a formal process. It received more of our attention because it deserved more of our attention. People loved it, and it was actually changing lives.

Ultimately, Nick would get to the point where he would strongly encourage employees to work on their "I Want To" lists. He would have them fill in the blanks: "I want to have_____," "I want to do _____," and several more. Nick would sit down one-on-one with employees to guarantee their goals were written down on the list.

He'd ask, "Okay, what do you want to have?" or "What do you want to do?" This is where he would consistently, time after time, get a blank stare. These employees would look back at him like he'd asked them to write out some kind of chemistry equation or something. Most had no idea.

But as they would start working through the list, they would became more and more empowered and focused, and eventually Nick would get them to a point where they were individuals who were pursuing life—not just reacting to it.

We want our employees to pursue things in their personal lives. To us, the professional and the personal life go hand in hand. Why do so many companies try to pretend that they are separate and that they should be kept apart? I look at Lance's letter in the following pages. In this letter, the guy just flat out says he disagrees with this concept, and so does Cellular Advantage.

Is the 9 a.m. Meeting for real? Has it helped us live our purpose statement? Is it significant? Have lives been impacted? Yes, yes, yes, and yes!

Here are some comments from some of the participants:

*After working in corporate America for close to a decade, I became aware of what was and was not politically correct to discuss at work. Employees are very guarded with what they share with coworkers and superiors in order to uphold the veil of perfection in their lives. Admitting problems or weaknesses was a sure ticket to the back of the promotion line. Talking about bills, financial issues, or anything related to dreaming of something bigger and better would have resulted in blank stares of amazement that you had gone off your rocker. Anything more than idle small talk about the kids and how great they were or how you could not wait until Friday and how the weekend had just flown by was too much information . . . and then along came Cellular Advantage and Nick Villotti. I met Nick at a church group and heard him talking about a 9 a.m. Meeting. At the time I was working for another company and assumed it was him rallying the troops and telling them what they needed to do in order to make him more money and be pawns for the company. Some time went by and I found myself out of a job because of the "economy." Long story short, I ended up coming to work for Cellular Advantage and Nick. My initial thoughts on the 9 a.m. meeting could not have been more wrong. Nick blows conventional thinking out of the water about how you treat employees. He is more concerned with what he can do in employees' lives than what they can do to benefit him. Asking about dreams and desires was such a foreign concept to me, and taking time out of his day to help people map out how to get there was mind blowing. As an employee, the program shows Nick cares about your success and how to make you a better person. As a human being, the investment he makes in your life gives you faith in people. In a time when it seems like everyone in the world is out for themselves and couldn't care less about their impact on others as long as they get what they want, the program is such a breath of fresh air. I'm still in the early stages of planning out where I want to go and what dreams I'm going to get out of the program, but just knowing it's there and the investment in me that Nick has made is huge. I know anything that comes out in our meetings is confidential and there is no judgment. If I wanted to go to the moon, I know Nick would come up with a plan to get me there. I cannot recommend the 9 a.m. Meeting enough. You truly get out what you put in. It's an awesome program led by an awesome person.*

**–Lance O.**

(This is a guy who moved on to a new career and also now owns a successful hair salon with his wife, a business plan that was a dream for them. They have been at it for more than six years, and they are looking at opening a second location. That is something that came out of the 9 a.m. Meeting, and that is something that makes us very proud. That guy did not work for us forever, as we suspected he wouldn't. And we could not be more proud of what he did when he left us. We also could not be more proud of the role we played in helping him achieve that goal with his wife.)

*The 9 a.m. Meetings were fantastic. It was a great idea reinforced by a great book (***The Dream Manager*** by Matthew Kelly). Not only did I learn and grow professionally from the experience, but I also opened my eyes to bigger and better joys in life!*

*I was kind of hesitant to set up the first meeting. Matt Fish, my manager at the time, told me that it was a good idea to at least try it out. I took his advice, and it went a lot better than I thought. I walked out of the meeting feeling ten times better than when I went in. Nick Villotti, my area manager, gave me a book to read—The Dream Manager. After reading the book, my mind ran wild. I started dreaming of things to do, places to go, and what I wanted out of my life.*

*After reading the book, I noticed an increase in my performance at work. My personal numbers started to go up, and in return, the store numbers started going up. My attitude at work changed. I was a happier person because I had something I was striving for. I was a more motivated person, wanting nothing but excellence. I was increasing my numbers, which sparked other coworkers to work harder, increasing the store numbers to a new high that I had not seen before.*

*I went into the first meeting not knowing what to expect and ended up changing my life. I owe this company more than words can explain. They have done so much for me, personally and professionally.*

*–***Mike W.**

*The 9 a.m. Meeting has changed the way many of our employees view their jobs. Many people go through the bulk of their lives without a plan. Because they don't have a plan, very often they can take that frustration out as dislike for their jobs. The feeling of "not getting anywhere" I think can become a way of life. At the most basic level, Nick listens and then explains that if you want different results, you're going to have to do something different than what you have done. This is scary and exciting all at the same time.*

*After discussing with Nick for a time some of the things I'd like to do with the rest of my life, I started to realize the amount of time I have is finite. I wonder how long I would have kept doing the same things that weren't leading to my personal success before I would have figured this out. I'm not saying I didn't have grand plans about the things I might want to do before I started the 9 a.m. Meeting. What the 9 a.m. Meeting has helped me to do is draw a map to where I want to be. Previously, those ideas were in line with the things people say they will do when they win the lottery.*

*For myself, I've always had a good credit score and paid my bills on time. However, my credit-card debt crept up over the last year. Every month I paid the most money on my largest credit card. Not surprisingly, the amount didn't decrease as much as I would have liked it to. Nick recommended a strategy of paying off the smallest debt first. Once that small debt is paid off, continue to pay more on the next-largest debt. Two months ago, I paid off a credit card I have had a balance on for more than a year and half. Paying off credit cards is the first of many personal goals, but most of my goals will require me to have money. This is just the start ...*

*–***Matt F.***

*The 9 a.m. Meeting is such a remarkably powerful tool for empowering employees at work, I felt like sharing what I have seen created by it. It can be life changing for our staff. Since Cellular Advantage has implemented the 9 a.m. Meeting, I have seen employees become more passionate about their lives and work. They bring a more positive attitude, a bigger drive, and a team mentality to work. I believe this is because the employees realize that the company wants to invest in them. They also share their dreams/goals with each other, and that helps hold them accountable. The amount of people that have never had anybody believe in them or stand by them and tell them they care about them is astonishing. I personally have had multiple people get extra emotional and tell me that nobody has believed in them and cared about them. This has moved me personally. Watching people that I care about being impacted so positively is what being a manager is all about. I truly feel that the 9 a.m. Meeting formulates a family atmosphere at work that can bring a win to everybody! Please keep running with the 9 a.m. Meetings. It has opened my eyes in believing Cellular Advantage is making a difference. I'm very proud to be a part of such a great company and their philosophy!*

**—Chuck R.**

*What the 9 a.m. Meeting means to me? Me time! It's the time where I focus on me and realize what I want out of life and my relationships—when I don't have to be afraid to say I took the wrong path and have the guidance to steer me back on course. To me this meant paying off debt, buying a new home, and having a plan where my financials are concerned. I am fortunate to have a good support group in my personal life and significant people who have taught me how to become a productive adult. However, it's hard to tell those people that the lessons they taught were lost because life didn't stop for me to take a breath! I am thankful that I had Nick to go to when I thought the hole was too deep. He helped me create a plan, held me accountable, and believed in me when he didn't have to. I never felt I was asking for help or admitting defeat; I just had someone to come alongside and make the journey with me.*

*Within the market I have seen people have similar successes in getting out of debt, buying homes, and creating new passions. The successes are infectious! With at least half of our market trying to become the best versions of themselves, our market has become a team of dreamers and believers. We want to share our stories, and we all become advocates for each other. Water-cooler talk is no longer gossip! We are asking what dreams we have accomplished and what we are working on now. We are more confident and productive in our personal lives and are more confident and productive at work!*

*—**Megan L.***

*The 9 a.m. Meetings have opened my eyes to a whole new view of the way I live my life. I now tell my money where to go through a budget that was put together during the 9 a.m. Meeting. Sticking to this budget has helped me get a new car and plan future dreams to accomplish. I've seen the 9 a.m. Meeting grow to new levels of participation, and as a result, our turnover rates are at an all-time low. This tells me people are happy to start working on reaching their dreams, and that helps Cellular Advantage, Inc. grow to new levels—growth not only in sales and revenue but growth in people's lives, whether it be getting married or fulfilling their dreams. I hope the 9 a.m. Meetings will grow to include all markets and see more people take their lives to the next level.*

*—Tim S.*

*When I was asked to write about my experience with the 9 a.m. Meeting, I had no idea what I would write. To me, the thought of dreams was big and unrealistic, but then we had our sessions. I learned it's not the size of the dream—but just to dream and put them in action. So I started small. I cleaned my unruly basement, started to finish the basement (almost done), and went from owing on six credit cards down to one (and almost have that paid off). I now have bigger dreams and all because I've accomplished (or almost accomplished) my "smaller" dreams, and my "bigger" dreams don't seem so unrealistic. I'm willing to bet I wouldn't have gotten nearly this far without the program. It's not because I want to impress anyone or be able to show the program is successful; it's because of the support system. It's my boss and other coworkers who genuinely care about my progress and them achieving their dreams that continue to inspire me. I'm grateful, my husband is grateful, even my credit score is grateful. Thank you for everything!*

**–Stephanie T.**

*I just want to say I enjoyed the 9 a.m. Meetings. I think it is great that you care about us as people and not just employees. I also think that the meetings helped me find out things about myself, things I never really thought about much or had long forgotten. I am thankful that you gave me the chance to think about these things and put many of them into action.*

**–Jeff W.**

*The 9 a.m. Meeting program has been a godsend for me.*

*It is such a simple idea: figuring out your goals, writing down your goals, and tackling your goals. Such an easy concept, yet I never thought of anything like it myself. And I know I am not the only one.*

*Everyone has goals and aspirations in this life. The only thing that keeps people from achieving these goals is having the feeling of not being able to follow through or having a thought but sadly just pushing it aside.*

*Once again, a simple idea, but just getting my goals down on paper was a huge step for me. Having a constant reminder in writing and not letting things be pushed to the back of my mind keeps me focused.*

*There is no better feeling than being able to mark off one of the goals I set for myself. There is a sense of true pride when you can tell someone, "I'm tackling my dreams."*

*The program has also inspired me to ask everyone, "What are your dreams? What are you doing to tackle these dreams?" I enjoy getting those thoughts flowing for every individual.*

*Anything is possible, and I am proud to say I am living proof . . .*
  *– losing fifty pounds and maintaining my current weight*
  *– paying off all my bad debt*
  *– working toward being a better person all around*

*And this is just the tip of the iceberg!*

*I want my legacy to be as rich and as positive as possible, and I am well on my way! Are you?*

**–Mike S.**

*I am a single mother of a two-year-old little boy, and before this meeting, I always felt like I was the only one on this earth in this situation, and listening to your story really made me feel so much more secure. I always felt like I was running into dead ends and like there was no relief for my situation! Listening to you speak about it made me realize that I have so many solutions. Before, I used to keep a journal and write down all my expenses, and after a while I found that useless, so I had really given up. But the meeting really had me thinking again. Thank you, Doug, for coming out here and sharing your experience with us. I will see you again at the meeting in June!*

**–Ariana P.**

# Chapter Two Takeaways:

- Nick Villotti, one of our top leaders, came up with the idea for the 9 a.m. Meeting, and it ended up changing many lives and had the side effect of significantly reducing turnover in our business.
- The 9 a.m. Meeting and the transparency it facilitates helped us realize and communicate to our employees that we had been through a lot of the same issues they were currently going through.
- The 9 a.m. Meeting helped a great many of our people to solve problems in their lives and then figure out what they wanted because many of them had no idea what they wanted.
- Work life and personal life are not separate, and they should not be treated as if they are.

# PART II

## THE 9 A.M. MEETING

# CHAPTER 3

## THINK LIKE YOU'RE SIX

One of the books that Nick and I have both read is *The Dream Giver* by Bruce Wilkinson. It talks about how each of us was born with certain inherent dreams and things that we are uniquely created to be good at, to be strong at—things that we are just going to naturally enjoy more than other things.

One question in the 9 a.m. Meeting is "Let's rewind the clock and go back to when we were little. Let's think about when we were six years old. What did you want then?" The success of these meetings relies directly on the person running them and their willingness to be transparent about their own life, as Nick is. He says, "Here's what I wanted to do when I was six," and I think that then gives our people the green light to share these kinds of things from their personal lives. They see that Nick has opened up, and it makes it easier for them to do the same. This is where the real magic begins.

When Nick was six years old, he was going to be an NBA star. He was going to be an astronaut. He was going to be a cowboy. He was going to be a fireman. He was going to be a few other things, too. The sky was the limit. No one had told him yet that he could not do the things that he wanted to do. People generally don't tell anyone at age six that they cannot fulfill their dream. They say "You can't eat that" or "You can't stay up past your bedtime," but normally no one says to a six year old, "You can't be a magician" or "You can't be a princess."

The imagination is limitless, and I think that is one of the coolest things about being that age. Without even really knowing why, you believe that anything can happen. Anything. There is really no reason you can think of that it can't happen, because life hasn't beaten you down.

So Nick moves slowly into the topic. He starts by saying, "Where did you live when you were six? What was your environment like?" He tries to bring them back to that age—to the sights and sounds and smells of that time in their lives. Then he asks, "What were the things that you really dreamed about doing? What made you go, 'Hey, this is what I want to do'? What interested you in those things?" At that age, the list is full of a lot of fun and creative things—artists, super-heroes, ballerinas—because that is what you are drawn to when you are six years old. It makes perfect sense.

So they start jotting those things down and talking about them. And then Nick moves it forward to when they are just getting out of high school. He asks them, "What school were you in? Who were your friends? What was your situation like? Where did you live? Did you have a bike? Did you have a car? Did you have a moped?" He encourages them to go back to that age in their mind: the sights, the sounds, the feelings.

And then he asks, "What was your plan? What did you want to be? What did you want to do? What did you want to have? What did you want to become?" And the list generally gets a little bit more focused, a little bit smaller. Then Nick brings them forward to today.

Many of our employees are somewhere in their early to mid-twenties. So Nick says to these twenty-somethings, "Now today, right now, let's look at that list again. What do you want to be? What do you want to do? What do you want to become? And what do you want to leave behind?" Most of the time, Nick will witness the blank stare I referenced earlier.

Not having an answer can be a little overwhelming or even disheartening. It is important to let people know that the feeling is normal. Nick often says, "Hey look, you're not the only one who has felt this way. We've had a lot of people who've had the same kind of reaction as you just had, but the great thing is that this is the starting point of something really fun and cool going forward, and it is going to help you think about things differently. It is going to help you figure out what you want, and then it is going to help you get it."

Then the blank stare returns because so many of these folks have been told, "Oh, you can't do that." Maybe it came from their family. It could have come from friends. Brothers and sisters. Cousins, grandparents, classmates. You never know, but a lot of people have been told at some point, "You can't do this" or "You can't do that." It gets people into a reactionary, cautious way of thinking about life.

They might say, "Oh, well, my dad told me that I can't be a college basketball player. He said, 'Son, only a small percentage of people ever make it to play college basketball. You're on the second team here in high school. How's that ever going to happen?'" Those are the kinds of comments that really affect people. And guess what. Those types of comments actually did affect someone very involved in this process: Nick. People of influence in younger people's lives often don't understand how impactful their words are. Those words are heavy, and they can greatly influence the lives of the young people who take them to heart.

Nick dreamed of playing college basketball when he was in high school, but he was told that he would never make it. We will get into the details of that experience in the next chapter, but before we do, let's look at the bright side. Today, Nick uses that story to help others in the 9 a.m. Meetings. He helps people work past the negative feelings associated with those unnecessary early setbacks. He helps them get on with the business of figuring out what they want to do with their lives from this moment forward. And then he helps them do it.

# Chapter Three Takeaways:

- We all have great dreams when we are six years old. The problem is, we give up on those dreams when the world starts to beat us down.
- Most young people hear someone tell them that they can't do something, and it is often convincing enough for those young people to believe it.
- The blank stare that follows "What do you want?" is often a result of hearing "You can't do that" too many times.
- Figuring out what you really want out of your future requires going back to the beginning and remembering what you wanted at the start of your life and at other subsequent points. Life is a journey, and every day (and every thought) leads us to where we are today.
- People are never too old to dream.

# CHAPTER 4

## KNOCK DOWN LIMITATIONS AND BARRIERS

One way Nick connects with our employes is by telling them about the jumping fleas, nature's most gifted jumpers.

## The Story of the Jumping Fleas

Years ago, scientists decided to do an experiment with fleas. They wanted to figure out if their performance would be affected by their environment. So the scientists put the fleas in a jar, and they noticed that they could jump out of the jar very easily. They could get out of the jar at will. They could go wherever they wanted and do whatever they wanted to do. They were free to go.

The next thing the scientists did was put the fleas back in the container, and this time they put a piece of glass over it. Now, when the fleas jumped, they would smash into the glass. Pretty soon, the scientists observed, the fleas were jumping almost up to the glass but not quite all the way. They were not banging their heads on the glass anymore. They had taught themselves to not jump as high as they were able to jump in the first place. And their heads felt a lot better. Fleas are smarter than you might think.

Here is where the heartbreak begins. The scientists knew that the fleas had adjusted their jumping to compensate for the glass ceiling. So they decided to remove the glass and observe the fleas' behavior once again. Off came the glass and out came the rulers. The scientists wanted to see how high the fleas would jump if they were free once again to jump as high as their abilities would allow.

Sadly, the scientists learned that the fleas continued to jump only as high as just below the level of where the glass had been. The fleas were concerned about hitting their heads on something that was no longer there. So the fleas went from being nature's greatest jumpers, to getting "concussions," to now just being basically above-average jumpers. That is a huge waste of talent!

The lab experiment continued, and the scientists wondered if they could motivate the fleas to jump again, the way they were created to jump. They decided to put a little heat under the container. Now the fleas' feet were getting hot, and they were in that jar saying, "I've got to get out of here!" And all of a sudden, up and out they went. And the fleas, once again, were right back to where they were before—the worlds' greatest jumpers. They could get out of the jar and go wherever they wanted. They could do whatever they wanted to do. But what a tragedy it would have been if no one had turned up the heat on them. Many times people experience similar things.

People get "concussed" going through life. They are told what they can't do, and they are labeled by people around them.

# My Story

I grew up in an interesting family. My brother is eighteen years older than I am, and my sister is sixteen years older. My parents had two kids in two years, and then I was the happy surprise (if you want to call it that) sixteen years later. I would rather be known as a "surprise" than what I heard sometimes. I heard the word "mistake." It wasn't used in a hurtful way, but that word doesn't really carry any positivity with it. Even if I only heard the word a few times, the weight of it stuck with me my whole life.

The second piece of my puzzle came in fifth grade or so. This is when we all started taking standardized tests so that teachers and school administrators could figure out how smart we were and where we should be placed among our fellow classmates. I scored very high on those tests and got placed in honors classes. My mom saves everything. She's got my sister's tests and my brother's tests, and when my parents saw that my scores were better than theirs, they expressed how proud they were and encouraged me to participate in talented and gifted programs.

Well, as school continued, through junior high and into high school, my grades were never as good as my sister's or my brother's. So I heard, "But you're smarter than they are. What's wrong? Why are you achieving at such a low level compared to your brother and sister, who are not as smart as you are, so to speak?" At this point in my life, I latched on to my second identifier: an underachiever. So in my mind, I was a "mistake" and an "underachiever." Those were my "concussions."

I was a flea jumping into a glass ceiling, and every time I hit it, it told me that I was a mistake and an underachiever. Both were things that I didn't realize meant anything until we started growing our company. When we had our first child, my wife decided to stay at home with her, so I was the guy in charge of the business at that point. Four years of success were followed by the opportunity to grow.

In the 2002 expansion of our company, my wife said, "I'm going to come back into the office and try to help." Her intention was that we were in this together, and she was going to come in and pitch in however she could. It was as simple as that. But based on those concussions that I had received, what I heard or what I was feeling, was *You're the underachiever. I don't know if you can handle this. I better get back in there and make sure nothing gets screwed up.*

Those concussions of mine were the things that shaped me. They influenced how I would react to situations in the future. They definitely worsened the already-challenging situation that we were going through.

# Nick's Story

Nick received some concussions when he was younger, too. He is a very talented athlete. When he was growing up, he loved basketball, and at age twelve, he decided he was going to play in the NBA. That was his dream: to play in the NBA. "I'm going to play college basketball, and then I'm going to play in the NBA," he said. "It's going to be fantastic." After a particular basketball game, on a night that he had played a tremendous game, he was talking to his dad. It was either right after the game or on the way home in the car. He said, "Dad, this is so cool. I'm going to play college ball, and then I'm going to play in the NBA." And that is when his dad said, "You realize you're probably not, right? Only a fraction of a percent of all of the basketball players in the United States ever make it to the NBA. You should probably stop even thinking about that because it's not going to happen."

Nick cried himself to sleep that night because of what he had heard from his dad. So it was, again, a concussion, a limitation. Nick had heard that he was not going to be able to achieve what he wanted to or to make something happen in his life. Nick remembers the details of that night to this day. Being open to sharing these kinds of life experiences promotes the transparency that makes the 9 a.m. Meeting work. Nobody is perfect. Everyone has taken some "hits" at some point. The important thing is to identify them and to work through them going forward.

# Recovering from "Concussions"

Let's say there's such a thing as dog school, and one dog is really good at running, swimming, retrieving, and barking. He's getting straight As in all of those classes. But he's getting an F in tree climbing. The teacher says, "Hey, Fido, you have got to stay after school today and work on your tree climbing." In the following weeks, Fido works his tail off trying to learn how to climb a tree. He puts in an honest effort every time. But he is never going to be any good at it. It's just not a part of his God-given talents. He is just not built for it. Across the street, at the cat school, they're all great tree climbers. But every one of them is getting an F in barking.

How many of our staff have been told by their family members that they should get better at "climbing trees" when they are just naturally gifted at something else, like "swimming"? In the 9 a.m. Meeting, setbacks such as these are discussed and conquered. By filtering the discussion through the three stages of the flea analogy, we are able to communicate to them how naturally gifted they are at something—just like the fleas are—and how life, or that glass ceiling, which is called "the lid," has concussed them in some ways. They start to understand that everybody has different levels of concussions. Some people have multiple fractures. They might have broken bones. Other people have only a bruise.

In the end, they leave the meeting being reminded that the flea is still a great jumper, and it just needs the right motivation or the right vision to get itself out of the jar. The next step is to say, "Let's remove that lid now. Let's go back and really dig into those things you thought about when you were six years old. Let's go back to that time when you didn't have any boundaries, you didn't have any of life's concussions yet." It's a pretty powerful statement, and it's a pretty powerful exercise. The six-year-old list just continues to grow and grow throughout the process.

It isn't an easy exercise to go through, but it is a healthy one. The goal is to maintain a very safe environment, and again, I think that comes from Nick and his transparency. He says, "Look, this is what happened with my dad and me," and that sets people at ease.

# "Border Bullies"

A lot of people are hemmed in by their circumstances, whether that means someone telling them they cannot do something or someone else (like a dad with a drinking problem) preventing them from having a normal childhood social life. In *The Dream Giver*, Wilkinson calls these people "border bullies." When a person wants to move outside of his borders and become a new and improved person, there are sometimes people standing around the border saying, "No, no, no. You're not that person. You've got to stay in here, inside this border.

This is who you are. Don't think you can be something bigger or better than that."

Those border bullies ultimately do not want a person to grow and change and do things better, because if they do, the bullies will think worse of themselves and think, *Why didn't I do that?* Those border bullies are often responsible for the concussions, and the concussion discussion during the lesson of the jumping fleas is a key to some people figuring out, *This is why I am the way I am.*

# Realizing Potential

Ultimately, Cellular Advantage just wants to treat everybody like the person they can be. And this is just the first part of the process. People tend to identify with the flea story. We've had a lot of people say, "I never would have thought I'd learn something from a flea experiment, but that is totally me. I totally get it."

Once people understand what their concussions—or perceived limitations or barriers—are, then they can begin identifying what their natural gifts are and what they can do. As they remember what they loved and were good at when they were younger, their minds are freed to embrace their natural gifts and imagine the meaningful contributions they can make at work and in their personal lives.

# Chapter Four Takeaways:

- Everyone has talents, gifts, and things they are naturally drawn toward.
- Lots of people have been told or have had an experience that may tell them that they cannot or should not do or pursue some of these things. They've been "concussed."
- Identifying these concussions is healthy.

- Thinking back to when you were six can really open your mind up to what those natural-born talents, gifts, and desires were.
- These things can provide great energy if used correctly.

# CHAPTER 5

## LEARN TO PURSUE LIFE

O nce people understand that there are things they are naturally gifted at and interested in, we help them to see how those things can be used to provide a spark in their lives. Nick and I divide people based on two types of camps: those who are just reacting to life (Reactive Camp) and those who are pursuing life (Pursuit Camp).

Which camp do you fall into? Are you making things happen in your life, or are you just taking what life throws at you? Ask yourself, *Do I know where I'm going, or am I just reacting? Do I feel that the best that life has to offer is out in front of me, or do I feel like the best that life has to offer has already passed me by?*

Questions like those are asked to take the person's temperature. Where are they? Do they feel there are good things coming down the road, or do they feel they are just kind of existing and accepting whatever happens to them?

It is important for someone to be able to place him or herself in one of the two camps. It is usually pretty clear if someone is pursuing life or just reacting to it. The ultimate goal is to give people the tools to move themselves out of Camp Reactive and into Camp Pursuit.

Helping people see the significance of what is in front of them is very important. Why is a windshield in a car bigger than the rearview mirror? Because we want to see what is coming at us and be ready for it. Having the foresight to see if there is an accident ahead—or perhaps a great opportunity—is imperative in being prepared for whatever is coming. People should have a clear vision of it. The stuff in the rearview mirror is back there behind us, in the past. Depending on how fast we're going, it might never be seen again.

This analogy applies to life, too. Learning from the things in the rearview mirror but leaving them in the past is a choice. And that choice allows a person to move forward, actively pursuing what's out there in front of him or her. That's the beauty of the human mind—having the ability to choose what you're going to believe. You can either believe your best days are in front of you, or you can believe your best days have already happened and are behind you—which leads to a life of simply existing, taking what life throws at you.

Matthew Kelly, author of *The Dream Manager*, defines the Reactive campers as disengaged. They believe that the future will not be any better than the past and that they cannot do anything to impact it. Kelly defines the Pursuit campers as engaged. They believe that the future can be better than the past and that they can have an impact on it.

## Switching Camps

If somebody is just reacting to life (Reactive Camp) and does not feel there is anything they can do to really impact their future, they're not going to be motivated to do much of anything. Why would they? They just take what life throws at them and react to it. There isn't any motivation to get financially or personally healthy, which directly impacts their work performance.

But if that person chooses to change camps to Pursuit Camp, where they pursue some things personally, there is great potential for magic to happen. When someone is pursuing life, they believe they can have an impact on their future and that the future can be better than their past. They are excited to get financially and personally healthy, which translates into a more motivated member of the work team.

They will be in this mind-set:

*When I look at my week and I'm at work and I'm selling stuff, I'm now excited to ask for that referral. I'm now excited to add this additional item on. Maybe it's an accessory. Maybe a customer needs a hotspot to take with her on a road trip. Maybe she could use an iPad. If I do these things with each customer who comes in the door and two out of ten of them buy something extra from me, I'm going to make a few extra hundred bucks a month, which is going to turn into an extra $3,000 a year. Now I'm that much closer to whatever it is on my list that I want. A new car. A vacation. An engagement ring. Some extra money in my daughter's college fund.*

# The Power of Want

We have found that there is a direct correlation between someone's personal wants and dreams and their performance within our organization. When people want things, they perform better at work.

Period. That brings us back to square one. People's personal lives and work lives go hand-in-hand. We see this time and time again when people personally come alive on something. Everything adds up to them at that point, and they get a sense of clarity, a sense of purpose. They say, "That's why I've got to do what I've got to do here at work, because I need that extra $300 to get me out of debt that much faster." Or, "I need that extra $500 a month to do X, Y, and Z."

So when people begin pursuing something personally, they become more productive professionally—and that benefits us. But it starts with the personal side, and we are committed to helping people live richer, fuller, more rewarding lives. As a bonus, they work more effectively and productively for our company. Everybody wins.

Seeing people build their lists of things they want to pursue is one of the most fun parts of the process. Many times we actually help them build their lists. In *The Dream Manager*, Matthew Kelly talks about a dream list, which has twelve categories. Kelly has people write down anything that pops into their head in these categories.

These categories can literally have hundreds of items in them, which Nick and I have found to be a little overwhelming for many people. So we have simplified the dream list into an "I Want To" list. It's easier for people to process and simply asks them to respond to the following prompts:

I want to be . . .

I want to do . . .

I want to have . . .

I want to help . . .

I want to enjoy . . .

I want to leave _____ behind when I'm gone . . .

The "I Want To" list can contain anything one of our employees wants it to. It's their life, and we want to help them get what they want. It might not all happen overnight, or even in a year, but it's a list to stay focused on and to work at.

| Before I die, I want to... | | | | | |
| BE | DO | HAVE | HELP | ENJOY | LEAVE |
| 1 | | | | | |
| 2 | | | | | |

What's on my "I Want To" list?
- I want to go to a high-performance driving school.
- I want to play golf on the top fifty golf courses in the United States.
- I want to publish a book—and look at that, you are reading it at this very moment!

# The Wheel of Life

A lot of times there is a monetary component to the things people want to pursue. In other words, some of the things that people want are not free. These goods and experiences cost money. So the Wheel of Life diagram is used to help people prioritize their efforts so they can earn the means to achieve their wants. The Wheel of Life has a center point with eight spokes radiating out, with each spoke representing a facet of a person's life.

**Number one is physical environment.** This refers to the place where a person lives—their city or town, their house or apartment, their kitchen, their bedroom.

**Number two is career.** Where do you work? At what level do you work within that company? What stage is your career in on the longer timeline of your life? Is it satisfying?

**Number three is finances.** What condition are your finances in? How are you set for money now? What about long term? Is there debt that needs to go?

**Number four is health.** Some aspects of your health are beyond your control. But how is your weight? How is your diet? How is your exercise regimen? How do you feel?

**Number five is personal growth.** Do you want to learn how to play a musical instrument? Do you want to learn to speak Spanish or fly an airplane? Do you want to go back and finish college?

**Number six is fun and recreation.** Do you play sand volleyball at night? Or softball? Are you biking? Running? Do you write music or poetry? What do you do for recreation?

**Number seven is significant other.** What kind of a relationship are you in, if any? If you're in one, how is it going? If you are not in one, do you want to be?

**Number eight is friends and family.** How is your relationship with your parents, siblings, and cousins? How about your spouse and children? What kind of friends network do you have, and how often do you see the people in it?

# Using the Wheel

## WHEEL OF LIFE

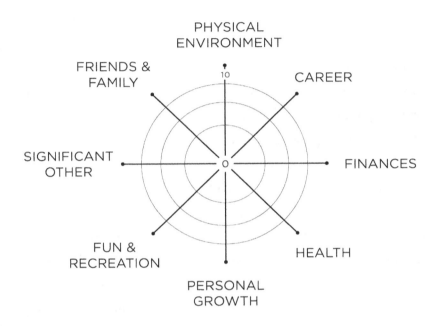

EXAMPLE OF
THE DOTS
CONNECTED

The next step is to consider each spoke and to place a value on each one, from zero to ten. The center point where all the spokes meet is zero, and the outer end of each spoke is ten. People are asked to rank each of the eight spokes according to how they think the things in that category are going currently in their lives.

For example, we'd ask, "Physical environment: How would you rate that from a zero to ten?" If you really love your living space, you might put a dot out at the end of the spoke—a ten. If you were unsatisfied with it, you might put a dot near the center—at zero or one. A guy might say, "Well, I'm sharing an apartment with two other guys and they're slobs, and they don't pay the bills on time. So, I'm giving my physical environment a three." In that case, he would put a dot less than halfway out to the end from the center.

Finances. The employee might say, "I've got some bill collectors calling. I'm probably carrying too much credit-card debt. I'm giving my finances a three." The dot would go in the same spot, closer to the middle than the end, but in the Finances slice this time.

Fun and Recreation. "Man, I have a great time. We're always doing something. Everything's great there. I'm giving that a nine." So, on that spoke, the employee would put a dot way out near the end.

This is done with every spoke, and in the end, there are eight dots. At that point, we have the employee connect the dots forming the "wheel." What kind of shape does that make? Does it look like a wheel? Would it even roll?

There are usually a few areas where the wheel is indented quite a bit compared to other areas. Those are obviously going to be spots on the wheel that are going to clunk along and not allow the wheel to turn very well because they are so low ranked. That is a wheel that is not consistent. It is "out of round." Maybe that person has "I want to go skydiving" as one of the things he wants to do or enjoy on his "I Want To" list, but going skydiving costs $400. If the Finances spoke on his wheel is a three because he is carrying too much debt, he has got a problem there.

At that point, he should probably question if skydiving should really be at the top of his list of priorities. We will encourage him to start choosing the things on the "I Want To" list that will create the best picture—the picture that he can focus on and work toward in the best way possible. The picture that stirs him inside, that creates energy, is the ultimate motivator. In the best-case scenario, he will say, "Oh, you're right. I probably need to fix finances first before I go and spend a bunch of money on other things."

# Ranking Priorities

There have been some light bulbs really turn on in people's lives. There was a guy named Steve who wanted to get engaged. He was carrying some credit-card debt. He knew that if he was going to spend a couple thousand bucks on an engagement ring, he was quickly going to be $5,000 in debt instead of just $2,500 in debt. So he decided that he was not going to get engaged until he had enough money to pay cash for the engagement ring. That was a goal that he set for himself.

Nick had Steve work the Dave Ramsey Financial Peace model. Steve is one of our top managers and top sales guys—he does very well with us. He just pounded out the debt, saved the money, and paid cash for the engagement ring. It is one of the coolest stories to come out of the Wheel of Life exercise. Steve painted a picture of what he wanted to do, and he kept his eye on that picture. We helped him with the tools, but he did the hard work—the actual work that was required to check that off his list.

It would have been pretty easy for him to go shopping and put an engagement ring on a payment plan or on his credit card. Instead, he got married debt-free, not $5,000 in the hole. Now he has a son, and his entire marriage and home life started out on the right foot, all because he got his finances in order—all because of the "I Want To" list and the Wheel of Life.

We have seen lots of people who are carrying too much debt get their eyes opened by the Wheel of Life. They see the Finances dot at zero, or even at three, and it helps them put things in perspective. It helps them look at their situation and say, "What do I need to focus on first? What's next? What's next after that?" It makes their goals manageable and understandable.

A lot of people think they have to fix everything all at once, and that can be overwhelming, paralyzing. It is therefore important to focus on making progress—not achieving perfection. This is done by choosing one thing to accomplish and taking the time necessary to get whatever that is done. It might take a year. It might take two years. But once that first thing is knocked out, you can then start to paint the picture for what's next. For our guy Steve, he could imagine standing there with his bride coming down the aisle, knowing he is starting his marriage with no debt. That is a pretty powerful picture, and to see him actually act on his vision and make it happen was really significant for us.

# Chapter Five Takeaways:

- People are either pursuing life or reacting to what life throws at them.
- Reactive Camp or Pursuit Camp are where people reside.
- How do people move from one camp to the other?

- The "I Want To" list is where our people start to figure out their personal goals.
- The Wheel of Life exercise helps us get all of the aspects of our lives into balance.
- We derive great pleasure in helping our people achieve their personal life goals because we know that life and work are connected and all part of the same experience.

# CHAPTER 6

## IMPLEMENT CHANGE

When the question is asked, "Do you like change?" the answer—probably nine out of ten times—is no. But then we say it another way: Would you like to wake up tomorrow debt-free? How about with a million dollars in the bank? Speaking a foreign language? Knowing how to prepare that gourmet meal? Being at your ideal weight?

Those are all changes. People see what we are doing and smile. "Yes, actually I do like change," is the new response.

What people do not like is the process of moving from where they are to wherever they need to be to make a change a reality. That is where discomfort and challenges set in. Getting people to move from an unhealthy lifestyle to a healthy lifestyle or to start saving money in order to create some wealth—whatever the case may be—is difficult, and that is the part of change that people so often try to avoid.

I made a big change in my life during the period when the "why" changed at home and at work. I decided to stop drinking. That was a big change. The new behaviors that came with that decision were all good, but the process was not always easy, and that is the part that people don't like—the process. They don't like having to add or drop things from their routines. "Transition" is the word used in *The Dream Manager*, and it is universally true that people do not like the transition period of any change.

## CHANGE CHART

### SUCCESSFUL CHANGE

### UNSUCCESSFUL CHANGE

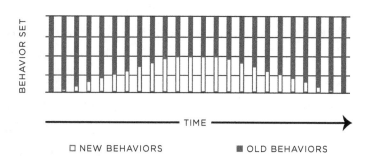

The vertical axis shows what combination of behaviors a person is doing. The horizontal axis is time. At the beginning of the horizontal axis, the behavior set is what is happening currently in that person's life. As time moves on, new behavior patterns are started, and some current behavior patterns are eliminated. Normally there is a fairly immediate change in what is added and subtracted due to the newness and excitement of starting to pursue something in your life.

It is normal to see a plateau where people get stuck. This is the hardest part of trying to implement change. In the diagram, we like to think the weight of the old behaviors is pressing down on the new ones, making it tougher for the new ones to become habits. It is in this plateau where many people slide back toward the comfort of what was normal and easy. Without a crystal clear vision of what you want—to provide the traction needed to keep moving up—it is easy to see a reversal in the graph. That clear picture provides the motivation to stick with the changes in behaviors that will equal lasting change!

As the graph begins to move up again, it is common to see the power of compounding kick in and the new behaviors gain momentum. The decisions we make have a cumulative effect, and at some point, the new behaviors outweigh the old, and the old can finally be put in the rearview mirror. When this happens, the line moves quickly up again. At the top, the change being pursued becomes a reality.

The plateau is the most crucial period in the process of moving along and up the curve. Without an extremely compelling reason to keep pushing on, the pull of what has always been comfortable is hard to overcome, and the weight of the old behaviors push their way back in, and the change isn't completed. The compelling reason is helped tremendously by a clear picture of what things are like when the change is complete. That is what provides energy!

# Developing a Clear Picture

One analogy that is used here is a TV with picture-in-picture. Imagine watching a sporting event on the main screen while in the corner of the screen—in the little picture-in-picture—a different game is on. What would cause you to actually change the channel to flip those screens? There has to be something compelling and exciting going on—a good reason for you to change the channel. Something that is boring and generic won't provide enough motivation to make the change.

That motivation—the promise of exciting things about to happen—is what propels people up the curve to real change. They must get clear on what those things are and how they can take steps toward getting them.

As I mentioned earlier, one of my goals is to play the top fifty golf courses in the United States. In my "I Want To" list, I've included pictures of Pebble Beach, Whistling Straights, Brandon Dunes, and Pinehurst, to name a few. One of my other goals is to play under par; I've got pictures and a video analysis of my swing in there as well. These are just a few things that keep me focused on my different goals.

Some of the things I want to be are a great husband, a great father, and a great friend. Those are kind of big-picture goals. What does it mean to be a great husband? Well, I've drilled down from there. For my wife to feel like I love her, I know that we should have lunch together once a week. We've got to have a date night every two weeks. And best case, quarterly, we need to have a getaway, just the two of us.

So, to be a great husband I need to do those things, among others. If I do those things, I know that she is going to be pretty happy as a wife—because I have learned what it is that she wants from me. I have learned what it is that she needs in order to feel like I love her. If we are out in a social setting, I know she'll want me to put my arm around her. She'll want to hold hands. She'll want to see that affection from me in public. That's important to her, so I've learned to give it to her. It is all part of being a good husband, and that is a priority of mine.

To be a great dad, I have built a Dad's Game Plan. As long as I am executing on that, I feel like I am probably doing a pretty good job as a dad. I am inevitably going to make some mistakes along the way, but that is unavoidable because I am human. The main thing is that I am dedicated to it, and I am giving it my best. That is everything.

To be a great friend, I want to be a genuine, authentic man. I want to be a great friend to a few people, instead of just having a bunch of drinking buddies. I would like to be friends with a smaller number of people so that I can have more quality time with each of them instead of being spread thinly among a larger group.

That is a look at some of the things that are on my list. When I look at "I Want To" lists of the people who work for us—the organization we affectionately refer to as the Island of Misfit Toys—getting out of debt is a big one. It shows up at the top of many of the lists we have seen. Buying a house, buying a better vehicle—those are definitely things that are also big with our employees. We are in retail sales, and it is not usually seen as a glamorous profession. Plus, a lot of our employees are on the younger side and in the beginning stages of their careers, so as you would expect, often their "wants" are very basic.

Some want to go on trips and vacations. We have had people who have never left the state of Iowa or the state of Nebraska. We have an employee in Hastings, Nebraska, who had never been to a University of Nebraska Cornhuskers football game, and that was on her list. She wanted to go to a Huskers game. We made that happen for her—U.S. Cellular is a big sponsor of Nebraska athletics, so that deal was an easy one to broker.

A rep in Southern Missouri wants to shoot a three-point basket at Allen Fieldhouse, where the University of Kansas Jayhawks play basketball. As soon as I heard him say that, I said to myself, "I know two people who can probably make that happen." So we are going to try to make it happen when basketball season rolls around. The rep said he did not care if he just went into the fieldhouse after hours and shot a three-pointer, but we are going to try to make it happen during a Jayhawks practice—we want to really blow that dream out of the water for him.

A lot of our employees' wants are money related—either getting out of debt or saving for something specific, whether a car, a house, or college tuition. We see some fun stuff from time to time—scuba diving and skydiving are pretty high up on some people's lists. We have also seen a lot of health-related wants. People want to lose a certain amount of weight, compete in a triathlon, or run a marathon—or even just a 5K race.

I've got a guy here in Des Moines who is big into the music world. He wants to see some of his own, personal music produced and then made available for someone to buy on iTunes. Our employees' wants vary so much from person to person, and it is interesting for us because we get to be a part of every single instance. We do everything we can to make these things happen for our people. And they reward us by working extra hard—for themselves as much as for us.

Our experience has shown that when people get a clear picture to move them up the curve, they draw energy from that. The picture usually concerns their personal life, and there is often a monetary piece to it. It is at this point that the dots get connected between their personal life and their work life. When they are pursuing something personally, the why of why they are going to work hits them.

# Meet Chuck

Chuck was 330 pounds when he started his 9 a.m. Meetings. He had worked for us at that point for ten years, and he was talking about how he was going to have to go to the sleep clinic in town to get help for his sleep apnea. Keep in mind that there is a great relationship between Nick and Chuck as you read his story.

Chuck is Nick's right-hand guy in running the Iowa market, and when Chuck brought up the idea of obtaining the sleep apnea machine, Nick said, "Chuck, you're going to do what?" Very matter-of-factly Chuck said, "Well, I'm going to go get fitted for a sleep apnea machine." Nick challenged him and called him out on it, basically saying, "You're not doing that." They ended up going into Nick's office to talk and closed the door. Nick said, "Chuck, you're not doing that. I can't sit here and support you on this. I can't let you get a sleep apnea machine because your sleep apnea is most likely directly related to how much you weigh. Let's not mask the real problem with a quick, temporary fix." Chuck got pretty emotional. He finally said, "You're right. It sucks." Then Nick said, "Well, what are we going to do about it?"

That was the day, I think, that Chuck decided that something was going to be different. Nick started going through an "I Want To" list with Chuck. He asked, "What are the things you really want?" One thing was that Chuck's parents had some cancer in their background, and Chuck thought he might have to fight through that himself someday. So he wanted to be healthy. He wanted to be around for his kids and his wife and ultimately enjoy a healthier lifestyle.

Chuck told Nick, "I want to make sure I'm around to help my kids grow up. I want to see my daughter get married. I want to see my son grow up and succeed." Chuck started imagining the future with his kids. Nick asked him to imagine what it will feel like when he walks Natalie down the aisle, what it will feel like when Nathan graduates from high school. What are those things going to look like, feel like? What year will it be when those things happen, and what do you need to do between now and then to keep yourself healthy so that you can be there for them?

These future visualization techniques painted a very clear picture for Chuck and helped him with a basic but very important concept: He could no longer stay at his weight of 330 pounds. He had to stay healthy so that he could be around for his kids and for his wife at these key moments in their lives.

Nick and Chuck talked through all of this, and Nick proposed a deal with Chuck. Nick said, "If you are willing to log all of your calories and exercise into this fitness tracker app, the company will pay for a YMCA membership for you so that you have a place to go work out. So the deal was made, and Chuck started doing it. He really changed his eating habits and his exercise habits through this process. And he never had to get the sleep apnea machine.

Every Monday, Chuck and Nick did a weigh-in together to track Chuck's progress, and soon enough, Chuck got to the point where he had lost eighty pounds. The next time Chuck came in for a weigh-in, he noticed a backpack sitting outside of Nick's door. Nick said, "Hey,

Chuck, will you bring that backpack in here for me?" Chuck reached over to grab the backpack and when he tried to lift it, he could barely get it off of the ground because it was so heavy.

When he lifted it, he said, "What in the world do you have in here?" Nick just looked at him and smiled. "That's how much extra weight you were carrying around five months ago." He had taken eighty pounds worth of weights and put them in the backpack. It was a pretty cool moment in Chuck's process. The process is never easy, but moments like this one make it all worth it.

As Chuck continued to drop pounds, at a certain point, he noticed he had a little lump in his neck. He went to the doctor, who sent him to an ear, nose, and throat specialist. It turns out there was something going on with Chuck's thyroid, and he never would have known about it if he were still three hundred pounds, because he would not have been lean enough to see or feel the lump in his neck. The doctors operated and took part of his thyroid out, and everything is good now. Who knows how that condition might have worsened if he hadn't noticed the lump. Having the courage to work through a change may have saved Chuck's life, literally.

Chuck made it down to 205 pounds. He is healthy and free of his thyroid problem. His kids are growing up. He is going to be there for them. He ran a half-marathon in 2013 and then a full marathon in 2014 on a team called "I Can," which is a group of people doing things they thought they couldn't do—like running a marathon, among many other things.

Chuck's story is a great one, and it all started because of a 9 a.m. Meeting where he and Nick sat down and started talking about life and answering the question "What do you want?" It is just a beautiful story—there is no denying that.

As far as the lesson of the jumping fleas goes, Chuck evidently had not had the right amount of heat under him to force him to jump out of the jar. When he started painting the picture about the things that he really wanted in his life and when that picture came into focus, all of a sudden things were exciting enough for him to change. He moved from Reactive Camp to Pursuit Camp. All of us could not be happier or more proud of Chuck.

## Tracking Progress

One of the early 9 a.m. Meeting attendees built an Excel spreadsheet to help people track their progress, with dates that progress to the future, from left to right. As you go down the page, it has spots where people can plug in items from their "I Want To" list—where they can say, "If I want to achieve _____ in sixty days, I have to . . ." It's a goal-tracking document. For Chuck, if he wanted to lose eighty pounds in a year, he would write in quarterly milestones that reminded him that he needed to lose twenty pounds every three months.

You just fill in the blanks. You do this by knowing your goal and considering the steps necessary to reach that goal. For somebody who wants to go back to school, that individual might say, "Thirty days from now, I've got to have my application in to Grandview College. Ninety days from now, I'm going to have my first tuition payment due of _____ dollars, so I need to start saving for that. In 120 days, I will actually start school, so I need to have this much money saved."

When people put the steps for achieving something on the "I Want To" list on the Excel sheet, it becomes a very useful visual aid. It helps them really see the steps necessary to achieve the thing they want to achieve. It also helps them see the order those things will happen in. They can see which goals are short term and which ones they can spend more time on. If Chuck's "I Want To" list included "I want to run a marathon" that goal would have been two years in the future. The goal in the middle, long before the marathon came along, would have been "I want to lose one hundred pounds."

This spreadsheet that we developed helps us set a schedule filled with milestones so that we can track our progress and stay focused on our goals. We don't just encourage our employees to use it—we use it ourselves. I use all of these tools and techniques in my own life, and it works for me as well as it works for our younger employees, many of whom are just starting their working careers and their "adult lives."

Personally, I want to get everything done all at once. I get overwhelmed pretty easily. Going through this process helps me break big things down into bite-sized pieces. When combined with the Wheel of Life, it is something that helps me realize, *That's just something that has to happen two years from now. No need to get worked up about it now. Here's the fun stuff I get to work on between now and then. Focus on progress, not perfection.*

Tom Allen is a man whom I have gotten to know pretty well. He is a dear friend and mentor to me.

He helped me view these things in big blocks of time. He said, "Doug, you've got from age forty-five to fifty-five, and then from fifty-five to sixty-five, and then from sixty-five to seventy-five. From seventy-five on, just call that bonus time." He really helped me look at things differently. I've got one hundred things on my "I Want To" list. I get to the point where I am almost paralyzed by the amount of things I have on my list. It is just how my brain works. Tom has helped me sit down and arrange these wants in an order that made sense. I am lucky to have him. I am also lucky to have the Wheel and our Excel spreadsheet. They are both great resources that help me settle down and do one thing after the other, all in due time.

We tell our people, "You can't do it all tomorrow. Make some progress. It is not going to be perfect. But by going through this process, you are ahead of 97 percent of the people in the United States because you have actually written down your goals, your desires, your dreams."

# Chapter Six Takeaways:

- Having a crystal clear picture of what you want in your life is a key to change.
- These pictures provide energy to keep moving across the plateau and up the curve.
- Change is a good thing.
- The process of changing is hard.
- It is easy to get partway through a change and get stuck on the plateau (or even go all the way back to what is comfortable).
- Having a clear and exciting picture of what the completed change looks like is the key to getting through the plateau and back up the curve.

# PART III
## RETAINING TALENT

# CHAPTER 7

## THE COST OF TURNOVER

Have you ever thought about how much it costs you as a business owner to replace an employee once he or she leaves? Turnover is something that most business owners consider to be just part of having employees. Unfortunately, these numbers can be staggering. My desire is that you will really understand the importance of retaining good employees once you are finished reading this chapter.

Integrating all areas of a person's life—personal and professional—has been a tremendous game changer in our retaining good people while helping them achieve their life goals. Of course, there may be different strategies or variations of our strategy that work for you and your company—but the bottom line is this: keep your people with you. Reduce your turnover. It could save you millions of dollars—*literally millions*. Sound inflated? Wait until you see the numbers for yourself.

Historically, at Cellular Advantage we have taken some of our top people from each of our markets and gathered them together for leadership training. It is called "Top Gun." A few years back, in 2009, we got a Top Gun class together and went to dinner the night before the first day of leadership training. I put a piece of paper at each place setting with the number "$704,000" on it. That number, that dollar amount, was the only thing on the piece of paper.

I let everybody know that the next morning they would have to come to the meeting with some kind of an idea of what that $704,000 represented. I got a lot of puzzled looks. Most of the people were not quite sure what to think about it. Regardless, we got through the night, enjoying a nice meal and some laughs, and turned in early so we would be fresh in the morning.

When our Top Gun leaders arrived and settled in the next morning, I said, "All right, what does the $704,000 represent?" I was ready to write down everybody's great ideas as to what the number represented. Instead, I looked out at a room full of blank stares. Some of those expressions might have been connected to people's hesitance to speak up rather than their lack of ideas—people can be shy about big numbers like that, especially when the number is probably connected to their employer's interests. But eventually people started to speak up. "It's our sales number," they said, or "It's the company's profit number."

I even got the comment, "I think it's the amount of money that you've spent on cars over your lifetime." The room started to have some fun with it, but ultimately, when we were done with the guessing and the teasing, I said, "That's my estimate of what employee turnover cost us last year."

Everyone went silent and just kind of looked around the room at one another. Then they looked back at me with expressions that said,

"Seriously?" I broke the ice by saying, "Well, that's an estimate." The group then went on to spend the first half of the day going through an exercise that would help us really figure out what the number was. I said, "Let's sit down and work this thing through as a team because I want you to be the ones who give me the real numbers. I want to make sure that we are all comfortable with what that number turns out to be."

So the team sat down and went through a couple of exercises. After a little research, we found some data on a uniform services company called Cintas. At the time of our research, they had a workforce of about thirty-three thousand employees and a turnover of about eleven thousand employees that year. Roughly 30 percent of their staff turned over that year. They estimated that the turnover cost them $110 million, which translates to roughly $10,000 per person. The second company in the research was U.S. Bank. They had fifty thousand employees company-wide, and their turnover rate was around 30 percent as well. Just like Cintas, U.S. Bank estimated that the turnover cost roughly $10,000 per person, for a grand total of $150 million in 2009.[1]

As our class continued reading, we found a call center, which may be more comparable to our dynamic at Cellular Advantage from a staffing standpoint. There were no retail examples, which was unfortunate. But the call center was a better comparison. It had 160 employees—20 administrative staff and 140 employees on the phones—and an annual turnover of more than 500 percent! They were hiring and rehiring roughly 47 percent of their staff monthly—a veritable revolving door of new hires. They obviously had huge cost numbers associated with their turnover.

---

1 Matthew Kelly, "The Turnover Dilemma: Keeping Employees by Fulfilling Dreams," http://changethis.com/manifesto/38.02.Turnover/pdf/38.02.Turnover.pdf.

From there, I turned the room's focus to Cellular Advantage. I said, "You've got my estimate, $704,000, but now let's build it as a team. " I told the assembled Top Gun leaders that there are costs that are easy to see on a financial statement, and there are costs that are difficult to see.

For our exercise, the group focused on two "hard" costs, which were easy to see on a profit and loss statement, and two "hidden" costs, which obviously were not so easy to see. Our first hard cost was the cost of recruiting. We looked at how many people were in the recruiting loop and what percentage of their typical week was spent recruiting. In our business, some of our store managers and some of our directors of sales attend job fairs. How much time are they spending there, and what is that costing us? We have had great luck getting people from the food-service industry to come and sell for us. One of our people might be out to lunch or dinner in a restaurant and notice a particularly personable server. They might strike up a conversation, and the next thing they know, they are having coffee or lunch and talking about a possible job at Cellular Advantage. That whole process costs us money. It is worth it, but it costs us money.

The second hard cost is the cost of training. What does it cost us to train these employees, these new hires? There are two costs to consider there—the cost of the new hire, and the cost of the employee who is doing the training.

Next, the group moved on to hidden costs, the costs that are not so easy to define. Lost productivity is the first one. The person who is training people cannot be doing something else, something that would more immediately affect our bottom line. What could they have been doing had they not had a new hire to train? Lots of things. Selling phones, for one thing. So there is some lost productivity there.

The other piece of that puzzle is the new employee himself, even after he has been trained. What level of efficiency is he operating at? Is he operating at 50 percent productivity in month one? How many months will it take to get him operating at 100 percent productivity? How long will it take to get him to operate at the level of the person he replaced? How long will it be until his manager can turn him loose? How long will it be until his manager can get back to doing the things he or she was doing before this new hire came on board? Those are the things to look at when talking about lost productivity.

The final piece of the puzzle is another kind of hidden cost. What does our business lose out on in terms of opportunities? If we had a veteran, home run-hitting salesperson in the store, she would be bringing in huge numbers for us, ringing up sales left and right. How much better would she be than a brand new, recently trained salesperson in the store? What does our business lose in referrals? Do we lose in repeat customers who would have been coming to our store to see that veteran salesperson specifically? Our veteran sales-people have a better set of sales skills and close a higher percentage of sales opportunities. How does that compare to someone who is brand new, tentative, finding his legs, and doing the best he can? It makes a huge difference.

That day, our Top Gun class considered all four of those costs—the hard costs of recruiting and training and the hidden costs of lost productivity and lost opportunities. Then I turned the group loose to figure out what those things added up to, dollar-wise.

They started off with the recruiting costs, adding up the cost of the recruiting ads themselves. Some of the people in the room had actually had experience placing some of our ads, so they knew exactly what those ads had cost us.

Then the group talked about the actual people cost. How many people are involved in the recruiting process, and what percentage of their time is actually devoted to recruiting? We figured out that our business had thirteen people in the recruiting loop and that roughly 20 percent of their time—about eight hours per week—was devoted to recruiting. So if thirteen are devoting 20 percent of their time to recruiting, the average person involved in that process costs us $35,385 dollars per year. We did the math, adding the advertising number to the recruiting number, and came up with $104,000 that could be tagged to recruiting costs on an annual basis.

Next, the group calculated the second hard cost: training. We figured out how many hours a new hire was going to be involved in preliminary training. This includes the time when managers aren't comfortable putting new hires out on the sales floor or letting them open a store on their own. During this period, new hires always have a ride-along person with them. They are on a continual learning curve and must take skills tests to assure us that they can handle themselves.

As a group, we decided that it takes eighty hours of actual training to get a new hire ready, to the point where a manager would feel comfortable letting him work with a customer on his own. We took that eighty hours and estimated that the new hire would be working for $9 an hour. In 2008, our company hired 111 people. So, doing the math, 111 people times eighty hours of training per person at $9 an hour got us to $79,920 in new-hire training costs.

Of course we could not forget to add in the cost of the trainer. Everyone agreed that the person doing the training would be earning $15 an hour. Repeating the same equation, this time using the $15 an hour figure, gave us a total cost of $133,200 for the trainers. We now had $104,000 in recruiting, new-hire training costs of just under

$80,000, and new-hire trainer costs of around $133,000. Adding those figures up gave us a hard costs subtotal of $317,120.

But the group still had to calculate the hidden costs—our lost productivity and lost opportunities. The entire class talked about what level of productivity a new hire operates at when he is just starting out. The consensus was that a new hire would be operating at about 70 percent productivity in his first month.

Our estimates showed that by month two, the new hire would get to 80 percent productivity, and by month three he would be at 90 percent. By month four, a new hire is really operating pretty close to 100 percent, the group decided, so we just assigned 100 percent to month four. We chose a conservative pay rate of $12 an hour and calculated the costs of lost productivity based on 160 hours of work in a month. By month four, when the new hire is operating at 100 percent productivity, this exercise becomes a nonissue. Using only the first three months—months in which the business clearly suffers lost productivity every time it hires someone new—we ran those numbers. They added up to $1,152 per employee in lost productivity.

Multiplied by 111 (our number of new hires over the course of the year), that $1,152 per employee became a total of $127,872. We added that to our $317,120 to reach yet another subtotal of $444,992. It was all starting to make sense to our staff, almost all of whom had stared at me blankly in amazement just a few hours earlier. In just a short time, with just a handful of calculations in our Top Gun training session, we had already come up with nearly a half a million dollars in employee-turnover costs.

The next piece of the puzzle was to talk about what happens when the star salesperson of the store is not actually in the store. What happens when the newbie is in his place? How much is that going to cost the store? This idea generated quite a lot of discussion.

How many sales is this person going to lose in his first three or four months because of how new he is? How many transactions is he not going to be able to close because he does not have good closing skills? How many customers are going to walk out of the store without buying something because they feel like this guy does not know what he is talking about? Is the newbie going to miss out on ten sales over the first four months? Or fifty?

Finally, after much debate, we agreed that over that first four months of getting a new hire up to speed and on his feet, our company would miss out on twenty sales, or roughly five per month. At that time, our average transaction was worth about $150. So if the company lost twenty sales at $150, times 111 hires, that was another $333,000 of hidden costs. We took that new subtotal and added it to the others, and our new grand total of turnover cost per year was $777,992. That is more than three-quarters of a million dollars, and that is just for one year. Our business could expect to lose the same amount, if not more, the very next year.

I had estimated $704,000 in losses, and the number our people came back with, after their calculations, was $777,992. I thought my number was bad, but theirs was even worse! In a completely separate exercise, I had our human resources director do research of her own to come up with yet another figure based on all of the same criteria. She used a government-agency formula, which included annual wages and benefits (which we had not considered in our exercise), and her employee-turnover cost came out to be $8,151 per person, or a grand total of $904,761 per year. The numbers kept getting worse, but they were all bad. Employee turnover is costly, and that is the bottom line. This exercise really opened a lot of eyes in our company. The numbers were scary—a low of $704,000 to a high of $904,000—but they were important to know, important for our people to grasp.

| | | |
|---|---|---|
| Recruiting Costs | $ | 104,000.00 |
| Training Costs | $ | 213,120.00 |
| Increased Overtime | $ | - |
| Lost Productivity | $ | 127,872.00 |
| Lost Sales / Opportunities | $ | 333,000.00 |
| **Total Turnover Costs** | **$** | **777,992.00** |
| | | |
| Quantity of new hires: | | 111.00 |
| **Cost per new hire:** | **$** | **7,008.94** |

**Recruiting Costs:**

13 people involved in recruiting loop. Approx 20% of their time. $35,385 annual salary x 20% = $7,077 x 13 people = $92,000 + cost of advertising. Advertising costs estimated at $1000 per month.

**Training Costs:**

80 hours of training per new hire. $9.00 per hour for the new hire and $15 per hour for the trainer. 111 people hired.

**Increased Overtime:**

There are some costs here related to additional overtime for staff covering store hours created due to someone leaving. We left the number at zero due to not having a good feel for it.

**Lost Productivity:**

After 80 hours of training at what level is the employee operating? We estimated 70% in month 1, 80% in month 2, 90% in month 3, and 100% in month 4. Assumes a $12 per hour rate and 160 hours per month.

**Lost Sales / Opportunities:**

The impact of having a new sales rep on the sales floor compared to a veteran is estimated at 20 lost transactions per person while the rep is getting up to speed. $150 per transaction is the assumption. 111 new hires.

If a company lost $777,992 in inventory etc..... I'm guessing someone would notice and it would be priority number 1. Why don't companies treat turnover the same? Why is it just considered a cost of doing business?

But again, the numbers are sometimes hard to grasp, so I put it in very real terms for the folks at Top Gun. I gave them a tangible example. "We hired 111 people, and they cost us X dollars," I told them. "What if today we lost 111 iPads or iPhones or Galaxy phones at $500 a piece or more? Our inventory manager would lose his mind."

If those phones were to go missing, some people would lose their jobs. That kind of inventory shrink would be completely unacceptable. We generally do not lose a single phone, but if we were to lose 111 of them, I guarantee there would be a lot of red flags and a lot of alarms going off in the CFO's office. Our inventory manager's office would be in panic mode. It would be all hands on deck.

But when that same amount of money (or potentially much more) is lost due to employee turnover, corporate culture is programmed to just accept it. "That's just a cost of doing business," you will hear people say. When our Top Gun group did the exercise and put actual numbers on our losses, it really opened our eyes. We started looking at what causes people to leave.

# Chapter Seven Takeaways:

- There are two types of turnover costs: costs that are easy to see on a profit and loss statement and those that aren't.
- Many companies tend to view turnover as a normal cost of doing business.
- Those same companies would have a cow if they had missing property totaling even a portion of the turnover cost.

# CHAPTER 8

## WHY PEOPLE LEAVE
## (AND WHY THEY STAY)

The research we found said that the number-one reason most employees voluntarily leave companies is that they have a bad relationship with their manager. Number two is that they do not feel like they are valued. Number three is that they do not feel their talents are being utilized—they feel they could offer more but do not have the opportunity to do so. Number four is that they do not have a way to measure their success. They do not know if they are succeeding or failing.

When Nick and I received this information, we referred once again to Matthew Kelly's *The Dream Manager*. Kelly says the biggest reason people leave their jobs is that they cannot see the connection between the work they are doing and what they really want out of life. Connecting those dots is where the power comes from. People want to work to live, not live to work. People who know why they go to work get much more out of it than people who just punch the clock. For us at Cellular Advantage, it all comes from the "I Want To" list. Our people say, "I'm going to work because I want to do, have, be, and experience these different things."

That takes us back to the whole idea of pursuing life versus being reactive. Why did Tiger Woods overhaul his golf swing three different times in his career? Why did he have the work ethic that he had? Because he wanted to win more major tournaments than Jack Nicklaus. Tiger Woods had a big "why." He had a clear picture to keep him moving forward. He had a dream and a goal. Think about Martin Luther King Jr. doing his big "I Have a Dream" speech. It wasn't "I have a strategic plan." It was "I have a dream. I have something with a really big purpose that reflects what I see in this world and what I want to do with my life." We just want to help our staff dig into dreams of their own and connect the dots between why they go to work and what they want out of life. When people can move from a paycheck-driven life to a passion-driven life, everyone wins.

Our examination of the high cost of overall employee turnover, using the numbers from that Top Gun meeting, started a conversation about employee turnover per market. At that point, we had stores in Iowa, Illinois, Missouri, and Nebraska. We took a look at new hires by region in 2008. There were 111 new hires company-wide that year, and we broke that number down by each of the four states. When we looked at turnover percentages, Nebraska was at 119 percent, Illinois at 107 percent, Missouri at 100 percent, and Iowa was way down the scale at 26 percent. Iowa had been at 86 percent turnover. It went from 86 to 26 percent and later went down even further.

So I asked our assembled people in the Top Gun meeting what they thought was causing the huge difference in Iowa. Why were so many people there sticking around and staying put in their jobs? Do they sell more there? Do they make more money? Are the Iowa stores busier than the stores in other states? What is it? The people from every state except Iowa weighed in with their professional business opinions on the reasons for the difference, such as "We're new to Chicago and new to Omaha, and it will take some time to catch up to the Iowa market and be as stable as they are there," and "The Joplin, Missouri, market is a lot smaller than Iowa"—and many others in this vein.

Then the Iowa people spoke up. Yes, the Iowa market was the most established of the four, and yes, reps generated more commissions in Iowa because of it. But that is not the reason people stay in the Iowa stores of Cellular Advantage, they said. The reason was the culture and the way the 9 a.m. Meeting impacts it.

One of our people in Iowa named Stephanie got up and told the group about how she had left Cellular Advantage because she had an opportunity to make more money at a different job. Six months later she came back because she missed the culture at our Des Moines office. She actually gave up money to work in an office that she liked better. The conversation then turned to the 9 a.m. Meeting and what that was all about. The Iowa folks spoke up and talked about how great the program was.

We then asked the people from the other markets what they thought about it all. The director of sales from Chicago was more of a traditional sales manager personality, and he said, "Let's get the numbers, let's get the numbers." I think he would have been uncomfortable in a 9 a.m. Meeting, and that is fine. It is not for everyone.

But it was a natural thing for Nick to do here in Iowa, where he was director of sales.

The 9 a.m. Meeting had not been available in Nebraska, Missouri, or Chicago, so for anyone who was interested, we offered a little taste of it right there at the Top Gun seminar. People got to build a small "I Want To" list, and then they were on their way. It was a big thing for some people. Two wanted to buy a house. One wanted to travel, one wanted to do a remodeling project at home, and one wanted to buy a boat for his mom. Four people said, "I want to get out of debt." Four wanted to increase their savings. Two wanted to save for retirement, one a new motorcycle, and one to go back to school. Building a kid's college fund was an item on one list, and two people wanted to give money to help orphanages for children. The "wants" were all over the place, and they were wonderful. It was like we had opened the floodgates.

We tried to help them connect the dots that day between what they want out of life and why they go to work, and we saw some pretty cool things. At the end of that meeting, we discussed how energy is the most important commodity in life. Everyone has energy. It is invisible, like electricity, but it is powerful. I asked them, "Where do you get your energy?" The answer I offered them is that "it comes from pursuing things, from going after things."

Your energy is generated from being in motion. It feeds off of itself. In the brain or the body, as long as you are in motion and pursuing something—as opposed to just sitting back and letting everything come at you—you will have energy. You will feel it. Our energy levels are directly and immediately impacted by our own motion, our own desires.

A Harvard Business Study revealed remarkable statistics related to goal setting and success:

- Eighty-three percent of the population does not have goals.
- Fourteen percent have a plan in mind, but the goals are unwritten.
- Three percent have goals written down. [2]

Everyone does not have a Cellular Advantage "I Want To" list, but the 3 percent of people who have simply written down what they want out of life are way ahead of the game. They have built a plan, or at least thought about a plan, to get what they want—to live the life that they have imagined.

That is how we have done things at Cellular Advantage. We have given people the tools to help understand themselves better, build their lists, and then the tools to help make it happen, step by step. Every day, ultimately, it is their choice to go after those things or sit back and take what life throws at them. If they choose to go after the things they want, that makes them happier in their lives and happier at their jobs. It translates to good things for us and, just as importantly, good things for them.

Checking things off of their lists becomes a habit. It becomes a way of life. There are always things that need to be done in order to move a life from point A to point B. It takes a certain amount of time before doing those things becomes ingrained. But after a while they become habit, and suddenly a person's whole life is in motion and energized—all for the better.

It is very easy to get partway through that process and then get stuck. It is just as easy to fall off. Anyone who has made a New Year's resolution to exercise and get in shape knows how easy it is to just quit. Health clubs are generally the busiest in January, then a little less busy in February, and then back to normal by March. But

---

2 "Goal Setting Facts," personalplan™, http://www.personalplan.com.au/2_Personal-Plan/Goal_setting_Facts/index.html.

what about the people who really stick with it—the ones who keep showing up in March and April, and all year long, and in the years to follow? They are the ones who have painted the clearest, most inspiring picture, and they receive the biggest rewards.

We try to keep our people motivated to stay on track, and ultimately they take over and keep themselves motivated, focused, and energized. It is an amazing program, and it has done wonders for our people and our company. These folks, I tell you, are on fire.

For me, this is the most fulfilling part of being a business owner—when I hear these stories and I see people grow. I see these people get turned on by something they had never thought about before—or something they had not thought about in years that they had given up hoping for long before. Consider a child whose parents could not afford a musical instrument. Maybe because of this, at a certain age, that child buried the dream to play an instrument. Well, through this process, that child—now an adult—can dig up that dream and resuscitate it. It is never too late. The next thing you know, that person is taking guitar lessons once a week and making real progress. When I see something like that happening, I think, *Significance.*

A lot of people never got any encouragement at home when they were growing up, and we try to offer as much of that as possible. I like to borrow an idea from my friend Tom Allen. He says, "I try to treat someone as the person they could be." So you forget for a moment about the person they currently are, or the person they think they are, and you focus on the person they could be—the person they want to be.

Do I want to make a great living owning a company? Sure. There are so many risks that go with owning a company that there had better be some rewards. I am absolutely in this to take care of my family and have a nice lifestyle. But a priority I would put even above that is a call to action that is best described from *The Dream Manager*: "How do we help people become the best versions of themselves?" This is important to consider because everybody is going to be unique, everybody is going to be different. And ultimately, the best version of a person is also going to be the best employee he or she can be, right? That is surely reason enough to do everything you can to keep your employees happy. That is *significant!*

# Chapter Eight Takeaways:

- Unfortunately, the high cost of employee turnover is just accepted in corporate America, written off as the "cost of doing business."
- If our company were ever to lose 111 phones instead of 111 employees, it would cause a huge uproar.
- If you invest into people, they will stay with you.

# CONCLUSION

Let me start this conclusion by saying that this program has really worked for Cellular Advantage. It is my sincere hope that these concepts have struck a chord with you and that you implement a version of the 9 a.m. Meeting within your business and that it gives you as much reward as it has given us. But I also know that it is not for everyone, and I am not here to tell you that you absolutely must do this. If you believe in it, do it, and you will reap the rewards. I truly believe that.

Ultimately, what we want to do is live our company purpose statement, "To enrich the quality of life for our own and our customers at each interaction." As a bonus, we noticed that our employee-turnover numbers went from 86 percent to 26 percent in one year.

Hopefully, in reading this book you will come up with some ideas of your own. Nothing in this process is set in stone. As you have read, we have added ideas from many sources to enhance our own little system. It is constantly evolving, and even though it is very established at this point, it is always a work in progress. Whether you choose to implement these ideas or not is your call. Your business is different than ours, but if there is anything we can do to help you put these things to work for you, we are here for you. We would love to help.

I look back to the original days of our business, and the idea was to have a successful company. Mitzi and I ultimately wanted to have a company that could run itself—a company we did not have to be involved in every single day of every single week. But what did we *really, truly* want?

I know that I wanted to be successful. My ego wanted that success for some of the wrong reasons. I wanted to be a big deal. That ego and greed drove our business so close to the edge that it was easy to see how terribly it could end. Changing the "why" painted that clear picture of what we wanted the future to look like. On the personal side, my marriage was a mess, too. My warrior wife, a new faith, and new priorities have taken our marriage to new heights as well.

As business owners, my wife and I had to figure out what we really wanted and then make changes to achieve those things. By figuring out what our core values and purpose were and then living them, we were able to really see change take effect in both our personal and business lives.

Investing in our company's people and trying to help them determine what they wanted out of life was how we chose to serve them. Help them connect the dots and figure out why they get out of bed in the morning, what they are working for, what they are pursuing. Help them change camps, from reacting to pursuing. Our company consciously made that decision—*to help our employees with life.*

It is in the core values statement of our company: "To enrich the quality of life for our own and our customers at each interaction." It is important to note that our business puts "our own" before "our customers." We want to enrich the quality of life for both, but our own people come first. And that is why the 9 a.m. Meeting was born. The big question at our office is "What do you want?" When people look at us blankly, as they almost always do, we have a system in place to help them come up with the things that they want. The things are always inside our people. It is just that sometimes those things need a little coaxing to come out.

It is an interesting concept, isn't it? "When you were six years old, what did you want out of life? What were the things that you thought you could do before life labeled you and told you that you had to fit into a certain box?" It is a question that everyone can revisit once in a while. At Cellular Advantage, we want our people to know they can be who they want to be. They can live the life they want to live. And we will provide them the tools to help make it happen.

Helping them determine those things, or to voice them if they already knew what they were, is a very early step in getting them out of the Reactive Camp, just taking what life throws at them, and into the Pursuit Camp, pursuing life on their own terms. Our people get a great deal of benefit from this program—but so do we. Everybody wins.

That is our story. I truly hope you were able to pull value from reading it and found something you can implement in your own business. If you would like any help with these things, we would absolutely love to help you.

I will tell you that our work environment is different than any work environment I have ever seen or even heard about. People's work lives and personal lives are connected. Our business embraces this fact and understands that we will not build a wall between the two. Turnover is inevitable—it happens in every company. There is good turnover, where someone leaves because ultimately the work or the company is not a good fit for them, and bad turnover, where someone "quits" but actually stays working at the place. Ouch. We have done a pretty good job of eliminating the latter kind of turnover, in large part due to our 9 a.m. Meetings and the exercises that stem from them.

Our company figured out a way to turn that $700,000 problem into a much smaller problem for us. And we keep working on it. By investing into peoples lives, we are impacting our business at the same time. It sounds like a cliché, but it is true.

For me, it all started with the eulogy in 2004. I was trying to figure out what I wanted out of life and how I could live a better life, a more purposeful and significant life. As most good things do, it snowballed, little by little, and here we are today. I would not have wanted to read what someone would have written about me if I'd passed away in 2004. In fact, there is a strong chance that no one would have written a single word about me. It's like the old saying goes, "If you don't have anything nice to say about someone, don't say anything at all." When I wrote the second eulogy that had me living to be ninety and making lots of changes to live a better life along the way, I got clear view of what I wanted. It helped me to see things written down. At that moment, I became part of the 3 percent of people who write down their dreams and goals. That is a good group to be a part of.

That eulogy helped me hone the vision of my life. It helped me ultimately boil things down to the one word, which was *significance*. Observing this period of transition for me, one friend told me, "The whole idea of being successful almost took a back seat to being significant." Then he looked at me and said, "You understand that they don't have to be mutually exclusive, right? Your success can be a blessing to other people if you do things the right way."

And it has. Since that day in 2004, I have been making sure that my calendar matches up with my plans, with what I want people to say about me when I am gone. I have been keeping my focus and living the life I want to live. I am staying true to my "I Want To" list, and I am making progress. Just today, I took an hour and a half out of the middle of the day to go watch my eleven-year-old son play tennis. That is me investing in the relationship with my son.

Soon I will be taking three days off to travel with our family to watch my daughter in an out-of-town dance competition. I will be present and engaged with those kids. I will be taking time off here or there to spend more quality time with my wife because I know that is what she wants. Things like that connect my dots and make a nice round wheel. All the while, as I am spending time with my family, phones and other devices will get sold in Cellular Advantage stores, and everything will run as smoothly as ever. Our employees will continue to live the lives they always imagined they could, and they will get one step closer to yet another major life goal of theirs. And so will I. We all will.